DONALD TRUMP

CENTENNIAL BOOKS

DONALD TRUMP

08

A WONDERFUL LIFE

Donald Trump's journey from New York City building sites to the White House is one for the history books.

CONTENTS

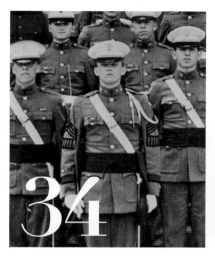

34

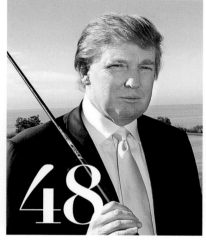

48

112

"NOBODY'S EVER DONE A BETTER JOB AS PRESIDENT."

He's a larger-than-life dealmaker, fighter, hero, villain and star. Everybody has a different opinion of Donald Trump, but one thing can't be denied: He's one of a kind.

The real estate tycoon defied all the experts by capturing the White House, and now keeps the world on its toes with a presidency that reflects his own outspoken style.

A self-described troublemaker as a youngster, Trump emerged from his father's shadow to make a fortune building glittering hotels, office towers, lush golf courses and opulent casinos, though his most successful creation had to be himself. He became the branded billionaire, with the glamorous wives, the jet-set lifestyle, the best-selling books and the hit reality TV show.

It all led to a stunning victory over Hillary Clinton to become the 45th president of the United States and a rollicking term with more drama than a season of The Apprentice. *It is an only-in-Trump's-America story with the stage set for a "Keep America Great" sequel.*

MAKING HISTORY
When Trump took office, he broke the record as the oldest incoming president as well as the richest and the one with the least political experience.

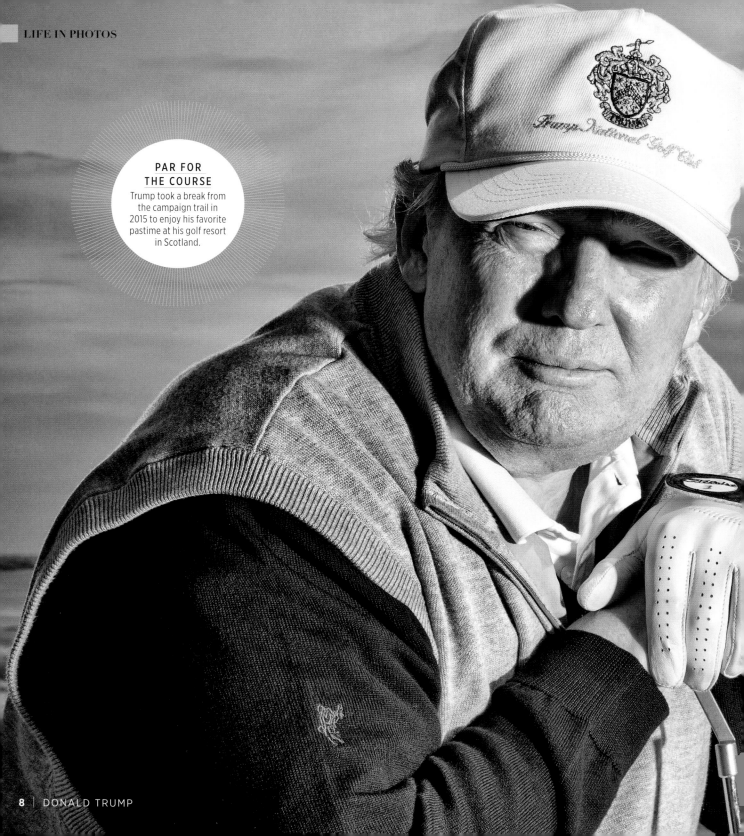

PAR FOR THE COURSE

Trump took a break from the campaign trail in 2015 to enjoy his favorite pastime at his golf resort in Scotland.

A WONDERFUL
LIFE

DONALD TRUMP'S JOURNEY FROM NEW YORK CITY BUILDING SITES TO THE WHITE HOUSE IS ONE FOR THE HISTORY BOOKS.

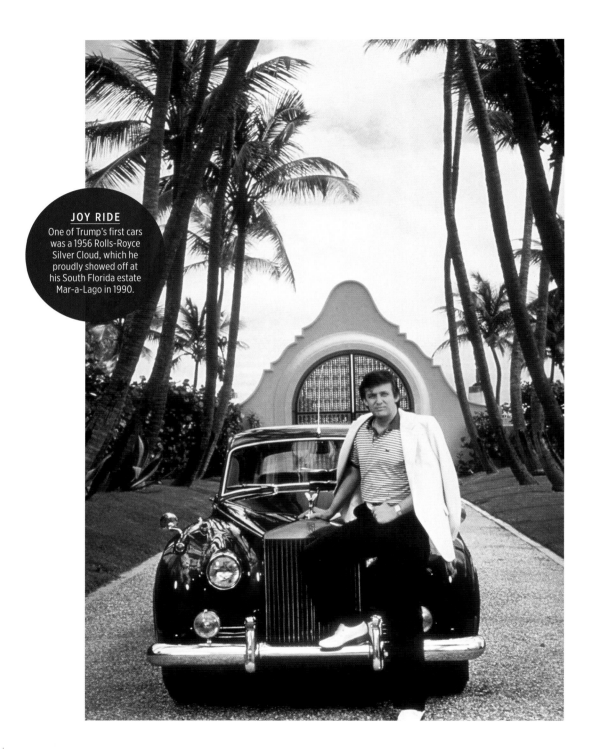

JOY RIDE
One of Trump's first cars was a 1956 Rolls-Royce Silver Cloud, which he proudly showed off at his South Florida estate Mar-a-Lago in 1990.

11

Donald and his first wife, Ivana,
were married for 14 years.

FLYING HIGH
Before Air Force One, Trump, seen here in 1988, got around in one of his three top-of-line Sikorsky helicopters.

Donald, Fred Sr. and then-Mayor Ed Koch celebrated the completion of Trump Tower on July 26, 1982.

"NEW YORK IS AN AMAZING PLACE WITH AMAZING PEOPLE."

DONALD TRUMP

ALWAYS WORKING

In 1987, Donald had a panoramic view over all of Central Park from his Trump Tower office.

Trump and first wife Ivana, here in 1988, owned a $29 million yacht called *Trump Princess* that was decked out with a pool, sauna, movie theater and elevator.

17

"I KNOW THAT WHATEVER HAPPENS I'M A SURVIVOR—A SURVIVOR OF SUCCESS."

DONALD TRUMP, IN 1990

He owned the Miss Universe, Miss USA and Teen USA pageants from 1996 to 2015.

DRIVER'S SEAT
Donald, here with daughter Tiffany and then-wife Marla Maples, takes a spin around Mar-a-Lago in 1997.

FIRST COUPLE
In 2011, Donald and Melania posed in front of their favorite spot at Mar-a-Lago.

Thank You, Lord JESUS, FOR PRESIDENT TRUMP

To Americans in Mobile, Alabama, Trump's presidential run was an answered prayer in 2015.

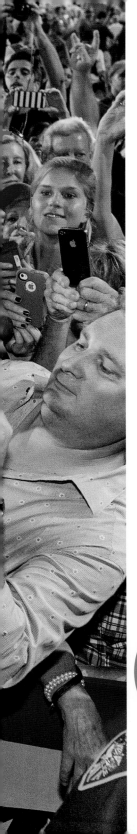

Melania, Donald and their son, Barron, joined the rest of the country in viewing the solar eclipse on August 21, 2017.

LIKE FATHER, LIKE DAUGHTER

Donald puts his faith in Ivanka, here together in 2018, as a trusted adviser. He says she's "a natural diplomat."

"NO DREAM IS TOO BIG. NO CHALLENGE IS TOO GREAT."

PRESIDENT DONALD TRUMP, IN A 2016 VICTORY SPEECH

Donald and Melania have been together for 21 years. "I have been aware of his love for this country since we first met," she said. "Like me, he loves this country so much."

The proud papa and his wife stand with four of his five children—Tiffany, Donald Jr., Ivanka and Eric—in April 2016.

"IF YOU'RE GOING TO BE THINKING, YOU MAY AS WELL THINK BIG."

DONALD TRUMP

Melania was right by Donald's side as he launched his reelection bid on June 18, 2019, in Orlando, Florida.

President Trump was welcomed by Queen Elizabeth II at Windsor Castle, where they chatted over tea in 2018.

29

HISTORIC DESK
The Oval Office's Resolute desk was built with oak from the *HMS Resolute* and has been used by nearly every president since 1880.

GREETING THE PEOPLE
Trump loves meeting his supporters throughout the country—and they love filling stadiums like this one in 2016 to hear him speak.

On January 20, 2017, Melania wore a stunning blue Ralph Lauren dress for her husband's inauguration.

**LEADER OF
THE PACK**
"In my own crowd, I was
very well-liked, and I
tended to be the kid
that others followed,"
Trump has said.

KING OF
QUEENS

★ ★ ★ ★ ★

THE SON OF A MILLIONAIRE, DONALD TRUMP WAS BORN WITH A SILVER SPOON IN HIS MOUTH, BUT REFUSED TO HAVE ANYTHING HANDED TO HIM.

IT'S NO COINCIDENCE THAT A MAN dedicated to making America great again was born on Flag Day, June 14, in 1946. Growing up in the New York City borough of Queens, Donald John Trump was the fourth of five children hailing from the wealthiest family in the neighborhood, self-made millionaire Frederick Sr. and his socialite wife, Mary Anne. On a tree-lined street in the bucolic Jamaica Estates neighborhood sat their castle: a two-story red brick mansion, six grand columns flanking its entrance. Inside, there were 23 rooms, including quarters for a maid and chauffeur, nine bathrooms, a state-of-the-art intercom system and one of the first television consoles on the block. Parked in the garage were his-and-hers luxury vehicles, Fred Sr.'s Cadillac limousine and Mary Anne's rose-colored Rolls Royce. Despite the outward opulence, "We had a very traditional family," Donald insisted in his memoir *The Art of the Deal*. "We were brought up to know the value of a dollar and to appreciate the importance of hard work."

The Trump children—Maryanne, Fred Jr., Elizabeth, Donald and Robert—had a shining example in their father, a real estate developer who made a mint building middle-

HOME SWEET HOME
The Trumps moved into this Colonial Revival mansion, built by Fred Sr., when Donald was 4 years old.

realdonaldtrump ● • Follow ...

4,441 likes
realdonaldtrump Who knew this innocent kid would grow into a monster? #TBT #Trump
View all 2,316 comments

realdonaldtrump ● • Follow ...

3,216 likes
realdonaldtrump #TBT With my family growing up—I'm on the left.
View all 328 comments

"We never thought of ourselves as rich kids," Donald (above, left) has said about his four siblings. From left: Donald, Fred Jr., Elizabeth, Maryanne and Robert.

income housing following World War II. Committed to growing his business, Fred Sr. worked seven days a week, often leaving the house before dawn and returning long after dinner. His idea of a vacation: "Two hours at the beach with us on Sundays, and he was back to work," Donald recalled in a 2015 *Rolling Stone* interview. Any quality time with their father would have to be on a jobsite, not a playground. Donald, the most business-minded of the bunch, often shadowed Fred Sr. as he made the rounds collecting rent. "He was a very smart guy, but very nuts and bolts," Donald told the *Washington Post* of

his dad in 2016. "No games."

Like her husband, Mary Anne excelled at her job. Described as "the perfect housewife" by her famous son, "besides taking care of us, she cooked and cleaned and darned socks and did charity work at the local hospital." The matriarch also kept her sons and daughters in line with a strict set of rules: They had an early curfew and were forbidden to use curse words, eat cookies, snack between meals and, for the girls, wear makeup. Anyone who disobeyed would be dealt with by their father, with punishments ranging from being grounded for days to being spanked

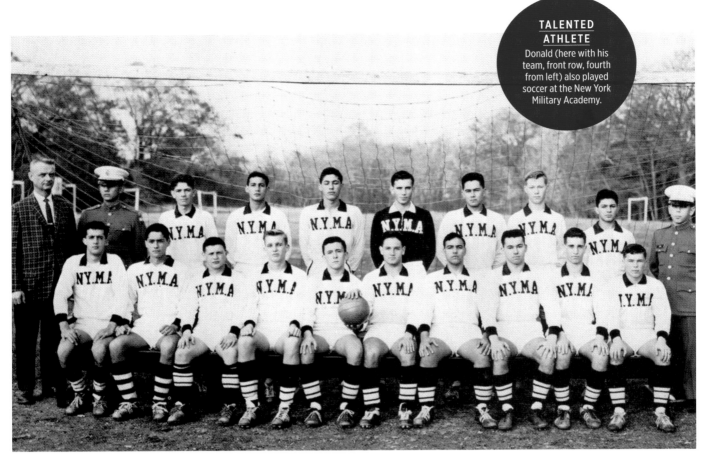

TALENTED ATHLETE
Donald (here with his team, front row, fourth from left) also played soccer at the New York Military Academy.

with a wooden spoon. As stern as she was, Mary Anne—who emigrated from Scotland to New York when she was 18—also had "a tremendous sense of pageantry," that Donald credits for his own showmanship.

Of his four siblings, Donald was the closest to Robert, two years younger and his complete opposite: Donald was blond, sturdy and confident, while scrawny Robert had dark hair and an introverted personality to match. The Trump boys would spend hours playing with their cars, trucks, model trains and, of course,

Donald with mother Mary Anne and father Fred Sr.

toy construction equipment. Because Robert was so easygoing, Donald often had a field day with his little brother. A favorite story of Donald's is the time the two were playing with blocks and he asked to borrow a few so he could complete a tall "beautiful building." Yet once Donald completed his structure, "I liked it so much that I glued the whole thing together. And that was the end of Robert's blocks."

At the private Kew-Forest School in Queens, Donald befriended a boy much like himself, Peter Brant, the heir to a paper-conversion company—and together they were double trouble. Classmate Fina Farhi Geiger remembers the jokesters being sent to the principal's office for throwing water balloons, shooting spitballs or pranking students with hot peppered gum and plastic vomit, gags they bought from a magic store during their subway joyrides into the city.

Donald was skating on thin ice, and one particular incident was the last straw. After Donald and Peter saw *West Side Story*, they wanted to be just like the Jets and Sharks and started carrying pocketknives. "We bought a little one, then a bigger one, and finally we were up to an 11-inch knife," reveals Brant. "There was nothing bad in it, we just wanted to…listen to the noise of flicking the blade." But once their parents learned of the dangerous hobby, "that turned Donald's father into thinking he should go away to school."

Fred knew exactly what institution could whip his 13-year-old "wise

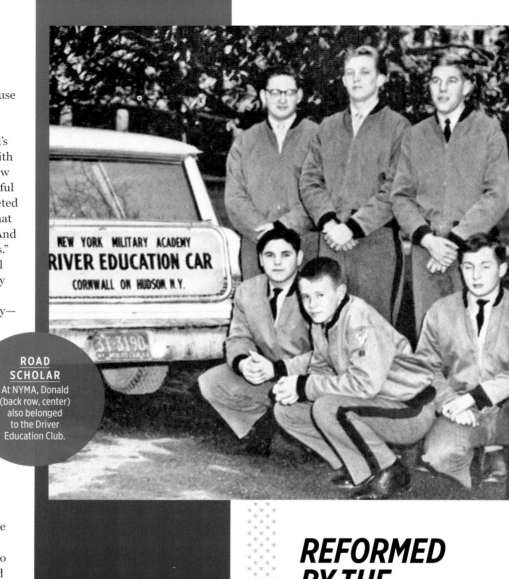

ROAD SCHOLAR
At NYMA, Donald (back row, center) also belonged to the Driver Education Club.

REFORMED BY THE MILITARY

As Donald entered his teenage years, typical behaviors like mouthing off and skipping school greatly concerned Fred and Mary Anne Trump—and

COURAGEOUS AND GALLANT
MEN HAVE PASSED
THROUGH THESE PORTALS

At NYMA, Donald (front row) excelled in the Honor Guard.

they acted swiftly to nip it in the bud. For his eighth-grade year in 1959, the 13-year-old was shipped off to boarding school upstate: The New York Military Academy. Designed to shape up wayward cadets through strict rules in an orderly environment, the school had inspections every Saturday morning; Donald would have to sweep, dust and clean his shared barracks, polish his shoes and shine the brass buttons, buckles and breastplate on his uniform. While most would find the chores repressive, young Donald welcomed NYMA's tight parameters: There was a contest for whoever had the neatest room, which played into his competitive nature.

"It's not an easy task for a boy away from home, having people barking at you, do this, do that, get in step, keep your mouth closed, take a shower, do your homework, go to bed, get up," noted Colonel Ted Dobias, the officer in charge of Trump's Wright Hall and his baseball coach. "Kids would burst into tears and beg to go home." Things were quite the opposite for DT, as his schoolmates called him. Nearly every weekend, his parents would visit, and they could see their son evolving—even more so, thriving. "The academy did a wonderful job," Mary Anne later revealed. "I would never have sent [younger son] Robert there; he was too sensitive. But Donald was different. He was never homesick, or at least if he was, he never let on. He loved it."

SMOOTH OPERATOR
Despite attending an all-boys school, Donald was voted Ladies' Man by his peers in his senior year.

guy" into shape: New York Military Academy, a boarding school founded by a Civil War veteran and run by drill sergeants 60 miles away from the Trumps' home. When Donald first arrived, "he didn't know how to make a bed," Colonel Ted Dobias told NPR. But by his senior year of high school, he had transformed into a bright student and respected athlete and was even appointed captain of the cadets, who in turn voted him Ladies' Man. After five years at NYMA, "I learned a lot about discipline," Donald admitted, "and about channeling my aggression into achievement."

After Donald graduated in 1964, he moved back into the family's Queens home while he commuted to the Bronx for business administration classes at Fordham University. But after two years, "I decided that as long as I had to be in college, I might as well test myself against the best"— and that was at the University of Pennsylvania's Wharton School. When Donald applied, he was up against 8,000 other hopefuls vying for one of 1,700 spots in the freshman class, but,

WHAT WAS YOUNG "DONNY" REALLY LIKE?

WHO'D HAVE THOUGHT THAT THE OVERLY CONFIDENT TROUBLEMAKER WOULD TURN OUT THE WAY HE DID? EVERYBODY!

Before he was The Donald, he was Donny, "very sharp and knew just what he could get away with," recalled Fina Farhi Geiger, his classmate at Kew-Forest School in Queens. "He had a reputation for saying anything that came into his head," added fellow student Donald Kass. Adults also noticed his bold personality. "He was headstrong and determined," one former teacher told the *Washington Post*. "He would sit with his arms folded... almost daring you to say one thing or another that wouldn't settle with him." Trump himself agrees, telling biographer Michael D'Antonio, "When I look at myself in the first grade and I look at myself now, I'm basically the same."

**FRED SR.
KNOWS BEST**
"I learned from my
father that every penny
counts, because before
too long your pennies
turn into dollars."

Like Father, Like Son

THE APPLE DIDN'T FALL FAR FROM THE TRUMP FAMILY TREE — FOR MANY GENERATIONS.

When Donald's father Fred Sr. was only 17, he joined his mother, Elizabeth Christ Trump, in the family's real estate business—and it later served as an example for his impressionable son, who began tagging along at construction sites from the time he could walk.

After Fred's own father died during the 1918 flu pandemic, the high school student traded extracurricular activities for night classes studying carpentry, plumbing, masonry and electrical wiring, and in 1923 he partnered with his mother (since he was still a minor) to create E. Trump & Son.

That same year, Fred began construction on his first property (as he continued his education at Pratt Institute in Brooklyn), which Elizabeth partially financed. Within three years, the 21-year-old had completed construction of 20 single-family homes throughout Hollis, Queens, including a row of seven on 199th Street, all of which boasted two stories, a decorative front porch, dormer windows, a driveway and garage— and sold for $7,500 each (approximately $110,000 in 2020). From there, he moved on to high-priced homes, building "authentic architectural reproductions" of English manor and Georgian Colonial five-bedroom, four-bathroom residences that sold for as much as $30,000.

When the Great Depression made it difficult to get loans, Fred shifted focus and opened a grocery store, Trump Market—yet his heart remained in real estate. And a decade later, during World War II, he returned to E. Trump & Son, building apartments for Navy personnel near shipyards along the East Coast. After the war, he turned his attention to middle-income housing for returning veterans, followed in 1964 by Trump Village, a cluster of seven 21-story apartment buildings situated on 60 acres on Coney Island. The largest project to date in Brooklyn, the $70 million residential complex was also the tallest, and could be seen from 20 miles out to sea.

As Fred grew his real estate empire, he always made sure to involve his business-oriented middle son, who considered him

Fred Sr. taught his middle son the tools of the trade.

to be his "most important influence." In his 1987 book, *The Art of the Deal*, Donald recalled, "I followed my father around to learn about the business close up— dealing with contractors or visiting buildings or negotiating for a new site.... I learned a lot from him. I learned about toughness in a very tough business."

as he boasted to *The Boston Globe*, "I got in quickly and easily." On campus, Donald stuck out like a sore thumb, with his sports coat and briefcase. In his real estate class, when students were asked why they had chosen the subject, he proclaimed, "I'm going to be the king of New York real estate."

Until then, the ambitious prince kept his nose to the grindstone. A teetotaler, Donald preferred studying to frat parties. And nearly every weekend, he returned to Queens to "work like a dog for his dad," recalled classmate Terry Farrell. Finally, after two years, Donald received his BS in economics, and although the degree didn't "prove very much" to him, he was excited for what was next. "The weather was beautiful, my parents were there," he remembers of his graduation ceremony. "The real beginning was that day."

America's Favorite Pastime— and Donald's

Trump had an affluent childhood, but he was just like any other American boy. He loved sports, especially baseball, and it consumed his free time. "We would go to stores together and look at the best possible mitt we could afford," recalls pal Peter Brant. "Our life revolved around watching the Brooklyn Dodgers play."

At New York Military Academy, the competitive teenager got to live the dream as a star first baseman with a .350 batting average—yet he was always eager to improve. "If you told him he wasn't throwing the baseball correctly, he'd do it right the next time," remembers coach Ted Dobias. "He was very sure of himself, but he also listened." And for all his hard work, he was rewarded during his senior year with the title of unofficial assistant coach.

"He was good-hit and good-field," Dobias told *Rolling Stone* in 2015. "We had scouts from the [Philadelphia] Phillies to watch him, but he wanted to go to college and make real money."

SPORTS BUFF 1 At NYMA, teenage Donald (at left) showed off a bowling trophy. **2** As the captain of the baseball team, "I played first base and I also played catcher," said Donald (in center). "I was a good hitter." He considered becoming a pro, but "I decided to go into real estate instead."

Donald, who'd gotten an
option on the site in 1974,
went to City Hall to reveal
his plans for the 34th
Street Convention Center.

WELL SUITED
From Trump Tower, Donald can see people enjoying Wollman Rink, "but I won't be one of them," he says. "Skating isn't my strong suit."

BILLION DOL

AFTER COLLEGE, DONALD TRUMP TOOK OVER HIS FATHER'S NEW YORK REAL

THERE'S NO QUESTION DONALD
Trump was cut from the same cloth as his father. Both men have a natural-born instinct for business, matched only by a relentless drive to succeed. But their differing generations also set them apart: Fred Sr., who made his millions in the wake of the Great Depression and World War II, was all about pinching pennies—while his son, an ambitious baby boomer, preferred to count dollar bills. And not long after Donald joined his father at E. Trump & Son in 1968, he realized affordable housing was not his passion.

LAR **MAN**

ESTATE BUSINESS—AND TURNED IT INTO A WORLDWIDE ENTERPRISE.

Not only were profit margins low, the budget was so tight there was no room for any of the design luxuries that appealed to him. Each property was just four walls—and lots and lots of economical red brick. Donald had "loftier dreams" and he didn't see them coming true in Queens or Brooklyn. He believed New York City was the future of the family business, but that would never happen as long as Fred Sr. was in charge. "You don't want to go to Manhattan," he told his son. "That's not our territory."

But it was where Donald felt at home. Since childhood, he had been drawn to the contagious energy of the city. And in 1971, in his early 20s, the Queens native made the move across the East River, settling into a cramped studio apartment on the 17th floor of a high-rise on the Upper East Side. Every morning, he hopped in his white Cadillac convertible and commuted to E. Trump & Son, which operated out of a dentist's office on the far end of Brooklyn. But once back in the city, Donald got around like a regular New Yorker. "I began to walk the streets in a way you never do if you just come in to visit or do business," he wrote in *The Art of the Deal*. "I got to know all the good

MADE IN MANHATTAN

A CLOSER LOOK AT THE NEW YORK CITY PROPERTIES THAT PUT THE TYCOON ON THE MAP.

GRAND HYATT
It was Trump's first major purchase, which he was only able to make because he worked out an unprecedented deal with City Hall to eliminate the hotel's sky-high property tax. "I went in and got the first tax abatement in the history of the City of New York," Trump said in 2016. "Nobody ever heard of a tax abatement.... It wasn't easy, let me tell you." In 1996, Hyatt purchased his half-share of the hotel for $140 million.

TRUMP TOWER
On the heels of the Commodore's success, Trump erected his first new construction: a 58-floor, all-glass skyscraper, the tallest of its kind in the city at the time. Over the three decades since, Trump Tower remains a staple of the NYC skyline and serves as the headquarters for Trump Organization. The family also lives in one of the mixed-use building's 263 residences: a three-story penthouse with views of Central Park.

THE PLAZA
One of Trump's few missteps, he was aware of the risk, but felt the prestige of the landmark hotel was worth every penny. "I have purchased a masterpiece—the 'Mona Lisa,'" he bragged in 1988 after snagging it for $390 million. "For the first time in my life, I have knowingly made a deal that was not economic." Trump was right: In 1995, the Plaza was sold off in a deal with Citibank and other investors.

DETERMINED
TO SUCCEED
If Trump's site
hadn't been selected for
NYC's convention center,
"I would have come up with
a third approach."

properties…but I still couldn't find anything to buy at a price I liked."

By the start of 1973, everything was falling into place. Fred Sr. had decided to step down as president of the company, handing over the reins to his son—who got right to work on his master plan. His first order of business was to rename E. Trump & Son to the Trump Organization. ("The word 'organization' made it sound much bigger," he later explained.) Next, he announced to *The New York Times* that the company was finally entering the Manhattan real estate market. Just one year later, Donald made the newspaper's front page: The Trump Organization purchased two waterfront properties on the West Side for $62 million

with the intention of putting up middle-income housing.

But when the city hit a fiscal crisis in 1975, all financing on new construction was suspended, leaving him with acres of land and no capital to develop it. Trump hadn't worked this hard only to fail now, and he quickly hatched a genius plan B: He proposed the 34th Street site for the city's new convention center. After years of negotiations, the deal went through for $12 million, with Trump earning an additional $833,000 broker's fee—which he offered to waive if they'd name the center after his family. "I've been criticized for trying to make that trade, but I have no apologies," he later said. "There wouldn't be a new convention center

Trump, here with ring girls, paid $11 million to host the 1988 Tyson vs. Spinks fight in Atlantic City.

"IF I HADN'T MANAGED TO MAKE ONE OF THOSE FIRST PROJECTS HAPPEN… I'D BE BACK IN BROOKLYN, COLLECTING RENTS."

DONALD TRUMP

WORDS FROM THE WISE

AS TRUMP'S BUSINESS EXPANDED, SO DID HIS WEALTH OF KNOWLEDGE — AND HE'S SHARED IT WITH MILLIONS.

Since 1987, the mogul has written an astounding 19 books, the majority on his best business advice. In his very first, the part-memoir *The Art of the Deal*, he revealed his "Trump Cards"— Think Big, Know Your Market, Maximize Your Options and Deliver the Goods—citing his own big moves in real estate as examples for each. *The Art of the Deal*, which spent 48 weeks on *The New York Times* Best Sellers list, sold 1.1 million copies at the time and

continues to be Trump's most profitable release: In 2019 alone, it earned him a cool $1 million.

Although Trump can be a braggadocio, he ate a slice of humble pie in 1997's *The Art of the Comeback*, in which he detailed his 1990 near-bankruptcy and how he bounced back thanks to negotiation. According to Trump, he asked for a $65 million loan to keep his business afloat until the market recovered and, "the banks more than capitulated—they

enthusiastically agreed to my proposal." He also shared his 10 tips to success, among them: Play Golf, Go With Your Gut, and perhaps his most personal as he was going through a second divorce, Always Have a Prenuptial Agreement.

Following his resurgence on *The Apprentice*, Trump focused on teaching others to be wealthy: 2004's *How to Get Rich*, followed two years later by *Why We Want You to Be Rich*, co-written

with *Rich Dad Poor Dad* author Robert Kiyosaki, which pushes entrepreneurship and investing in real estate over mutual funds. The two also share some unconventional advice. While Kiyosaki rejects "living below your means," Trump reveals that a friend would only fly first class, even when he couldn't afford it. "He needed it mentally.... It put him in a good state of mind and he became a very, very successful guy."

GRAND PLANS
Trump, here with NYC economic development administrator Alfred Eisenpreis, triumphed with his renovation of the Commodore Hotel.

in New York today if it hadn't been for the Trumps."

After revitalizing 34th Street, Trump moved up a few blocks to 42nd Street and Park Avenue. Located across from Grand Central Terminal, the Commodore Hotel was a shadow of its former glory: rundown, overrun with derelicts, and years behind on paying its property taxes. Yet the entrepreneur saw a diamond in the rough. Everyone else thought he was crazy. Even Fred Sr., chairman of the Trump Organization, told a reporter that "buying the Commodore at a time when even the Chrysler Building is in receivership is like fighting for a seat on the *Titanic*."

Still, he had faith in his son and granted Donald a small loan, as did the Hyatt hotel chain, in exchange for 50 percent ownership. And after a complete $100 million renovation, which included paradiso-marble flooring, brass railings and a 170-foot glass-enclosed restaurant perched over 42nd Street, Trump reopened the hotel in 1980 as the luxury Grand Hyatt, in a ceremony that was attended by New York Governor Hugh Carey and New York City Mayor Ed Koch. The project garnered the 34-year-old a wave of publicity and raised his profile as a Manhattan real estate developer—but more importantly, it impressed his father. "What do you think of what

my Donald has put together?" Fred Sr. marveled to a *Vanity Fair* writer. "It boggles the mind!"

Emboldened by the Commodore's success, Trump orchestrated a residential real estate takeover of Manhattan all through the 1980s: Trump Plaza, a 36-story apartment cooperative on the Upper East Side; Trump Place, a complex of 16 luxury high-rises that revitalized the West Side; and most notably, his crown jewel, Trump Tower, next to the Tiffany & Co. flagship store in Midtown.

The 58-floor, 28-sided structure with a signature stepped facade was the first of its kind when doors opened in 1984: On the ground floor,

Trump by the Numbers

FOR NEARLY 50 YEARS, HE BUILT HIS WORLD-RENOWNED BRAND—
AND THE DEPTH OF HIS PORTFOLIO IS NOTHING SHORT OF IMPRESSIVE.

$3.1 Billion
Net Worth

Approximately half of Trump's money comes from Manhattan real estate, with his national and international properties and brand businesses making up another $1.6 billion.

Hotels
Whether on the Las Vegas Strip, the Chicago River, the Waikiki shores or the woodlands of Aberdeen, Scotland, the award-winning Trump Hotels promise luxury accommodations and a five-star experience.

Aviation
The $32 million Trump Fleet boasts a custom Boeing 757 with 24-karat gold accents, a Cessna jet and three Sikorsky S76 helicopters for VIP guests in New York, Florida and Scotland.

Estates
Beginning with Mar-a-Lago in 1985, Trump represents a half-dozen of the world's most exclusive properties, with perks like 24-hour butler service, Waterford crystal chandeliers and a helipad.

Golf Courses
A number of Trump's 12 American clubs (valued at $210 million) have hosted PGA and LPGA tournaments; they're the model for his seven courses in Scotland, Ireland, Indonesia and Dubai.

Casinos
In addition to four Atlantic City, New Jersey, properties, Trump Entertainment Resorts managed Trump 29 in Southern California and Trump Casino in Gary, Indiana, before all eventually closed.

Winery
In the foothills of the Blue Ridge Mountains, Trump's Albemarle Estate in Charlottesville, Virginia, sits on the state's largest vineyard (worth $30 million) and produces 36,000 cases of wine each year.

Residential Real Estate
The majority of his holdings are in Manhattan (14), with nine elsewhere in North America and another 11 scattered across the globe in India, Indonesia and South Korea.

Food & Beverage
In addition to licensing apparel and home furnishings, Trump offered spirits (vodka, wine and beer), steaks and bottled water. Trump Ice, he said, was "so good people wanted to buy cases of it."

"MY FATHER TAUGHT ME EVERYTHING I KNOW."

DONALD TRUMP

"I created thousands of jobs and made a lot of money in Atlantic City, which was what, as a businessman, I am supposed to do," said Trump, pictured in front of his first New Jersey casino.

Atlantic City: A Gloriously Profitable Failure

THE CASINOS FLOPPED BUT HE STAYED IN THE GAME BY PLAYING WITH HOUSE MONEY.

Seven years after New Jersey legalized casino gambling in 1976, Trump wagered on Atlantic City, opening his first casino, Harrah's at Trump Plaza, in what would become a stormy partnership with the Holiday Corporation (owner of Harrah's); it ended with Trump dropping $70 million to buy out Holiday. Undaunted by the meager returns from what was now known as Trump Plaza, he purchased a partially completed hotel from the Hilton Corporation for $320 million, rechristening it the Trump Castle with then-wife Ivana as manager. He then picked up a third property, the under-construction Taj Mahal, in 1988, for $1.1 billion, much of it financed with junk bonds. Squeezed by debt and on the brink of personal bankruptcy, Trump's company restructured the loans with the bank, while keeping him as chairman.

Trump dropped out of the casino business altogether in 2009. But since he had put in little of his own cash, and even shifted some of his personal debt to the casinos, he emerged millions ahead. "Atlantic City fueled a lot of growth for me," he later told *The New York Times*. "The money I took out of there was incredible."

Trump stands outside the Taj Mahal in 1990.

a five-level atrium trimmed in marble and soaked in sunlight—which gives it a golden glow—features luxury shops, cafés and a stunning 60-foot waterfall wall. "Trump Tower was an unqualified success," boasted the bombastic businessman, who had a reported net worth of $100 million in 1982. "It had given me visibility and credibility and prestige. It was also a great success financially." Within three years, Trump Tower, which cost $190 million to build, had generated $240 million in apartment sales, for a profit of $50 million—in addition to the $10 million Trump personally earned in commissions as an agent.

Following the fanfare of his new Manhattan icon, he came to the rescue of a relic from the city's past. Central Park's famed Wollman Rink had fallen into such disrepair, it was shuttered in 1980 for a planned two-year $4.7 million renovation. But by May 1986, due to a comedy of construction errors, the project was $12 million over budget with no end in sight— until Trump stepped in with an offer Mayor Koch could not refuse: He would rebuild Wollman at no cost to the city within six months. In return, he'd assume operation of the ice skating rink, and once he recouped the money he invested, additional profits would be donated to local charities. "I have total confidence that we will be able to do it," Trump told reporters at the time. "I am going on record as saying that I will not be embarrassed."

And he wasn't: As promised, Wollman Rink opened its doors on November 1—two months ahead of schedule and $750,000 under budget. That day, before live TV cameras, the budding tycoon beamed as he cut the ribbon, flanked by Olympic figure skating gold medalists Dorothy Hamill and Scott Hamilton. In 1987, ticket sales at Wollman reached 250,000, double what they had been back in 1980. The project not only proved Trump as a fiscally minded businessman, but also hinted at his potential for cleaning up government spending.

Within a decade of entering the Manhattan real estate market,

"IF IT'S GOT TRUMP'S NAME ON IT, IT'S GOT TO BE THE BEST OF THE BEST."

AIRCRAFT INTERIOR DESIGNER ERIC ROTH

EVERYDAY LUXURY
In addition to his 757, nicknamed Trump Force One, Trump owns a small private jet and three helicopters.

Trump had conquered it. Where to next? More than 100 miles away in Atlantic City, a seaside resort in New Jersey best known for its beach and boardwalk. After gambling was legalized in 1976, developers rushed to put up casinos in the "Las Vegas of the East Coast"—and Trump was right in the thick of it. In 1984, he opened Harrah's at Trump Plaza, a 2.6-acre complex that boasted a 60,000-square-foot casino, 614 rooms and seven restaurants. Within minutes, "thousands of people poured in," he recalled. "They were lined up three and four deep at the tables and the slot machines."

Within two years, though, Trump turned over his share of the ownership to partner Holiday Inn and focused on his next Atlantic City projects: Trump Castle, a 15-acre resort with a 75,000-square-foot casino; and Trump Taj Mahal, which, at 120,000 square feet of gaming space, was billed as the largest casino in the world—but it was also Trump's largest sacrifice. As its budget ballooned to $1 billion, the entrepreneur was forced to sell off his Trump Shuttle airline and mega-yacht *Trump Princess* in order to finance it. (Trump Taj Mahal closed in 2016, five years after Landry's Inc. bought Trump Castle for $32 million and renamed it Golden Nugget.)

Trump learned from his mistakes, however, and after surviving the

THE MAN IN HIS CASTLE
Trump, pictured in his Trump Tower office in August 1987, spent long hours at his desk as he built his empire.

"MY WHOLE LIFE HAS REALLY BEEN A 'NO.' IT HAS NOT BEEN EASY FOR ME."
DONALD TRUMP

Michael Jackson and Lisa Marie Presley honeymooned at Mar-a-Lago in 1994.

SPENDING TIME AT MAR-A-LAGO

The 1920s estate in Palm Beach, Florida, that Trump picked up at a bargain-basement price in 1985—with then-wife Ivana Trump installed as overseer—has become the unofficial Southern White House. The oceanfront residence is situated on 20 acres between Lake Worth and the Atlantic ("mar a lago" means "sea to lake" in Spanish). Within the 128-room, 62,500-square-foot mansion, Trump has hosted world leaders and relaxed by playing on the members-only, 27-hole Trump International Golf Club course nearby. Built by cereal heiress Marjorie Merriweather Post, the mansion—with 58 bedrooms, 33 bathrooms and three bomb shelters —cost the equivalent of $90 million to complete in 1927. After Post died in 1973, Mar-a-Lago was willed to the U.S. government for presidents to host dignitaries, but it was returned to the Post Foundation in 1981 because of the high cost of upkeep. Later listed for sale for $20 million, the Post family couldn't find a buyer, as the estate had fallen into disrepair. Plans were made to demolish it until Trump picked it up for a reported $10 million, a fraction of the original cost. He then launched a full remodel, spending an estimated $10 million to add a 20,000-square-foot ballroom (where he and Melania held their wedding reception in 2005), tennis courts and a pool.

TRUMP'S BUSINESS HITS AND MISSES

★ ★ ★ ★ ★

HIT Grand Hyatt

Trump converted the creaky Commodore Hotel near NYC's Grand Central Terminal into the glittering Grand Hyatt, generating steady income and a $140 million payday when he sold his half-interest in 1996.

MISS Plaza Hotel

Trump's "Mona Lisa" frowned on his pocketbook, failing to generate enough revenue to cover the interest payments on the 1988, $390 million purchase. He sold the hotel in 1995, with the proceeds going to the banks instead of him.

HIT Trump International Hotel and Tower

Trump bought the seven-story *Chicago Sun-Times* building in 2004 for $73 million and turned it into a 98-story hotel and condominium skyscraper. Though he originally envisioned it as the world's tallest building, he scaled back the project after 9/11.

MISS Trump Vodka

Trump once imagined bar patrons ordering T&Ts—Trump and Tonics—but Trump Vodka, launched in 2006, was discontinued five years later.

HIT Trump Winery

Operated by Trump's son Eric, the former Kluge Estate Winery and Vineyard that Donald bought in Charlottesville, Virginia, in 2011 churns out 36,000 cases of wine a year and has picked up many awards.

MISS Trump Steaks

Buyers never developed a big appetite for "The World's Greatest Steaks," as Trump called them when they were launched in 2007. The exclusive distributor, The Sharper Image, took them off the market after just two months.

HIT Mar-a-Lago

Trump purchased cereal heiress Marjorie Merriweather Post's 1920s-era Florida estate in 1985 and converted it into a members-only golf resort originally run by then-wife Ivana. It now serves as his favorite presidential retreat.

EARLYSUCCESS

"When I renovated Wollman Rink in Central Park, it came in $750,000 under budget," Trump tweeted.

GETTING IN THE GAME
In 1983, Trump bought the New Jersey Generals, a team in the now-defunct United States Football League.

financial hit of Atlantic City, there was no looking back. The new decade ushered in an abundance of fresh business ventures. Back in Manhattan, Trump alternated between five-star luxury hotels (Trump International), residential high-rises (Trump Palace) and commercial skyscrapers, most valuably Trump Building. In 1995, he paid only $1 million for the vacant 72-story landmark 40 Wall Street located across from the New York Stock Exchange, renovated it for $35 million and transformed it into one of his most lucrative properties, worth upwards of $500 million. By 2020, the Trump Organization owned 19 pieces of real estate scattered all over Manhattan; *Forbes* estimates their value at $1.5 billion, slightly more than half of his net worth.

The end of the 1990s was the start of an entirely new enterprise for the Trump Organization portfolio: Trump Golf, "the world's best luxury golf experience." The businessman first picked up the sport during his college days at Wharton, and in 1999, he found a way to monetize his passion with the opening of Trump International Golf Club in West Palm Beach, Florida. Membership at the private 27-hole course, which also features a clubhouse lavish enough for weddings, costs $25,000 annually, in addition to a reported $150,000 initiation fee.

Over the following years, Trump added a number of golf properties to his portfolio, including his first foray away from the East Coast, a spectacular course in Los Angeles on 2 miles overlooking the Pacific Ocean. Following the U.S. financial crisis in 2007, Trump bailed out a number of struggling golf courses across the country by purchasing them—and adding his Midas touch and the Trump name. As of 2020, he's the proud owner of 19 golf resorts throughout North America, Europe and Asia, to the tune of $590 million.

With a reach spanning real estate, hospitality and entertainment, the Trump Organization expanded even further. In the new millennium, the Trump brand iteslf became the focus—and it was omnipresent. The famous name synonymous with luxury has been slapped on more than 50 different products, including everything from menswear and home furnishings to bottled water. (In 2019, *Forbes* reported that Trump's licensing deals make up $80 million of his net worth.) The American brand also popped up on holdings all over the world: Architectural masterpieces Trump Towers Istanbul and Trump Tower at Century City in Manila, Philippines, as well as restorations of iconic properties like Scotland's Turnberry golf resort, now known as Trump Turnberry.

TRUMP'S WORLD

THE PRESIDENT OWNS, OPERATES OR LENDS HIS NAME TO LUXURY PROPERTIES FROM MANHATTAN TO MANILA.

FROM GOLF COURSES TO skyscrapers to luxury hotels, Donald Trump's name graces properties around the world. Among his most profitable ventures: a Washington, D.C., hotel in a historic building leased from the federal government, and a golf course in Miami.

1 Palm Beach
The Mar-a-Lago Club is a members-only golf resort Trump purchased and renovated in 1985; he's called it his Southern White House.

2 Los Angeles
The Trump National Golf Club is an 18-hole, Pete Dye–designed public golf course in Rancho Palos Verdes that Trump purchased out of bankruptcy in 2002.

3 Chicago
The 98-story Trump International Hotel and Tower was completed in 2009 on the former site of the *Chicago Sun-Times* newspaper.

4 Las Vegas
The 64-story Trump International Hotel Las Vegas is a hotel, condominium and time-share skyscraper completed in 2008.

5 Washington, D.C.
The Trump International Hotel Washington, D.C., opened in 2016 in the Old Post Office near the White House after a $200 million renovation. A favorite of diplomats, it generated more than $40 million in revenue in 2018.

6 Miami
The Trump National Doral Miami is said to be the biggest

moneymaker for Trump. In 2018, the golf resort made $76 million in revenue.

7 New York
Trump's signature property, Trump Tower is a 58-story mixed-use building on Fifth Avenue, completed in 1983.

8 Hawaii
Trump International Hotel Waikiki, a 462-unit condominium and hotel tower, only licenses the name.

9 Ireland
The Trump International Golf Links & Hotel opened in 2002 and has a Greg Norman-designed course.

10 Philippines
The 57-story residential Trump Tower Manila licenses the Trump name, but isn't owned or operated by the president's businesses.

11 South Korea
Trump World Seoul is a Trump-branded collection of six condominium properties.

12 Turkey
The Trump Towers Istanbul are two conjoined towers—one offices, the other residences—owned by a Turkish billionaire who pays Trump for the use of his name.

13 United Arab Emirates
Trump International Golf Club, Dubai, is one of two projects Trump's company is involved with in the Middle East. Still under development, Trump World Golf in Dubai will feature a golf course designed by Tiger Woods, a world-class clubhouse and residences.

After five decades as one of the world's leading businessmen, Trump resigned from his namesake company to take on an even more colossal project: president of the United States. In January 2017, he turned over the billion-dollar Trump Organization to his three eldest children, Donald Jr., Ivanka and Eric (see page 96 for more), along with chief financial officer Allen Weisselberg. But it's not because he couldn't handle both jobs. "I could actually run my business and run government at the same time,"

"OWNING A GOLF COURSE GIVES YOU GREAT POWER."

DONALD TRUMP

Trump insisted. "I [just] don't like the way that looks."

The incredible journey from president of the family business to president of the country is one his

father sadly didn't live to see: Fred Sr. died in 1999 at age 93. "But I think he would've been amazed that something like this could happen," said Trump. "He would've been very proud."

PAR FOR THE COURSE
In 2005, Donald showed off his Trump National Golf Club Los Angeles, in Rancho Palos Verdes, California.

PLEDGE OF
LOYALTY
"All I can tell you is he's
been vicious to others
in his protection of
me," Trump shared
in 1980.

A Complicated Friendship

TRUMP LEARNED MANY IMPORTANT LESSONS FROM HIS MENTOR,
RUTHLESS ATTORNEY ROY COHN.

Famously known for his role as prosecutor for the House Un-American Activities Committee hearings over alleged "Communist sympathizers" infiltrating various aspects of American life in the 1950s, attorney Roy Cohn, by the 1980s, had built a reputation as a ruthless deal maker in New York City when he met the ambitious young Donald Trump. Cohn represented some of New York's most powerful businessmen, like Yankees owner George Steinbrenner, and a price he often demanded from his friends and clients was loyalty. That is just one of the lessons Trump, a quick-rising real estate scion, learned from the man who became his most important mentor. "He's a genius," Trump told writer Marie Brenner in the mid-1980s. "He's a lousy lawyer, but he's a genius." Despite Cohn's shady reputation, his strength and resilience appealed to the young Trump. "He was a prototypical Teflon man," former federal prosecutor Jim Zirin has written of Cohn. "He was the man to see if you wanted to beat the system." Cohn's tactics included tenets like "Never settle, never surrender; counter-attack, counter-sue immediately, [and]...claim victory and never admit defeat," author Sam Roberts told *Vanity Fair* in 2017. And Cohn, who died in 1986, once said, "I decided long ago to make my own rules." It's a philosophy that appealed to Trump, and he took his own version of that—draining the swamp and disrupting a dysfunctional government—to the White House.

TRUMP THE
STAR

HE ONLY PLAYED ONE PART, BUT HE PLAYED IT
TO PERFECTION IN A STRING OF CAMEOS. THEN
THE APPRENTICE CAME ALONG.

Trump's talking *Apprentice* doll said phrases including "You're fired!"

HE HAS A FILM AND TELEVISION résumé any actor would envy, even if his range, like his wardrobe, is severely limited. In a series of appearances spanning decades, Donald Trump played one role: Donald Trump. "Waldo, you're the best son money can buy," he tells his child in 1994's *The Little Rascals*. Like the antiquated cellphone he's talking on (it has an antenna!), the walk-on was vintage Trump: unapologetically rich and brash, a part he honed to perfection in real life, then parlayed into side gigs. There's The Donald looking like he's ready for a board meeting when Steve "Stone Cold" Austin smacks him to the mat at WrestleMania. And when he dons a tux to share a pizza with ex-wife Ivana in a Pizza Hut commercial, he's in full negotiation mode—business and personal—

Trump posed with Hulk Hogan at WrestleMania VI in 1987.

"Everyone thought he was this hilarious caricature," Megan Mullally said of Trump.

telling her she's only entitled to "half." Looking back, these appearances could all be seen as part of a continuum, a buildup to his longest-running self-performance as the host of *The Apprentice*, itself a successful audition for his biggest star turn of all at 1600 Pennsylvania Avenue.

Trump never stops selling—himself, his properties, his personal life—on the big screen. When he gave directions to a young Macaulay Culkin in *Home Alone 2* in 1992, they were in The Plaza, a hotel he owned at the time. And he previewed his future third wife, Melania Trump, in a red-carpet scene in *Zoolander* in 2001. One thing he couldn't sell: his acting chops. His 1989 cameo (again, playing himself) in *Ghosts Can't Do It* with Bo Derek landed him a Razzie

Award for Worst Supporting Actor.

Trump's long-standing faux-feud with WWE owner Vince McMahon culminated in 2007's "Battle of the Billionaires." Each picked wrestlers to represent them, but Trump took matters into his own hands with a "hostile takeover," slamming McMahon to the floor. And when his stand-in won, Trump gleefully helped shave McMahon's head in the ring.

Trump played his persona big (and for laughs) with a variety of TV cameos throughout the '90s, offering some unhelpful writing advice to a mayor with writer's block on *Spin City,* dropping by a New York penthouse to meet a fellow "zillionaire" on *The Nanny* and visiting Will Smith and his family in *The Fresh Prince of Bel-Air* (in the

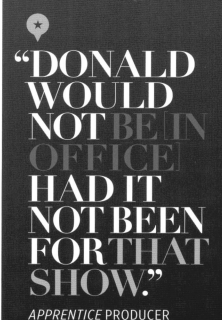

"DONALD WOULD NOT BE [IN OFFICE] HAD IT NOT BEEN FOR THAT SHOW."

APPRENTICE PRODUCER KATHERINE WALKER

Macaulay Culkin talks to
Trump in *Home Alone 2.*

"*THE APPRENTICE* WAS THE SINGLE BIGGEST FACTOR IN PUTTING TRUMP IN THE NATIONAL SPOTLIGHT."

TONY SCHWARTZ, CO-AUTHOR OF *THE ART OF THE DEAL*

episode, he jokes about liking to keep "a low profile," and is ready to do a cash deal for the California mansion).

For a bit at the 2005 Emmy Awards, Trump wore overalls and a straw hat, and held a pitchfork for an off-key, tongue-in-cheek duet of the *Green Acres* theme with *Will & Grace*'s Megan Mullally. (The actress even worked Trump Tower into the lyrics.) It gave him some country cred 14 years later when, as president, he tweeted the clip before signing a farm bill.

By the turn of the century, the Trump Organization was starting to plateau. Donald Trump, nearly 60, was at the age most people consider retiring. Instead, it seemed a man arguably past his prime needed to rebuild his company if it were to survive in the new millennium. Thousands of miles away, in the remote jungles of Southeast Asia, Mark Burnett was producing a brand-new competition show called *Survivor*. Who could have known the two were headed for a chance encounter that would earn each millions of dollars— and change the course of history in the process? With the success of *Survivor*, British-born Burnett was brainstorming how to duplicate the show on dry land, specifically in the cutthroat world of corporate America. "They've got to be working for someone big and special and important," he mused. But who? That person would soon be sitting in front of him at the

2002 *Survivor: Marquesas* finale. For the live broadcast of the winning tribal council, Burnett rented out a New York City landmark: Wollman Rink, which Trump famously restored to its former glory back in 1986. Nearly two decades later, the tycoon was sitting in the front row for the *Survivor* festivities and Burnett took advantage of the coincidence, buttering up the man he had in mind to host his new show, *The Apprentice*.

"Welcome, everybody, to Trump Wollman skating rink. The Trump Wollman skating rink is a fine facility, built by Mr. Donald Trump...Trump, Trump, Trump, Trump, Trump," Burnett recounted years later. His plan worked: Before the producer could even make his way backstage, Trump jumped up to shake his hand. He was even more flattered when Burnett said he had read *The Art of the Deal* as a young man selling T-shirts on Venice Beach and it changed his life. But convincing Trump to host *The Apprentice* would require all the negotiation skills he learned in the memoir.

At a time when reality TV consisted of *The Bachelor* and Paris Hilton's *The Simple Life*, Trump felt the category "was for the bottom-feeders of society," and he was a veritable businessman. But he also saw an opportunity to boost his sputtering brand. "My jet's going to be in every episode," Trump bragged to his then-publicist Jim Dowd. Even better, when *The Apprentice* premiered in 2004, Trump Tower was on full display each week as more than 20 million Americans tuned in to hear him tell unlucky contestants, "You're

Former *Apprentice* star Omarosa Manigault campaigned for her boss in 2016.

BYE-BYE, BEAUTIES
In 2015, Trump bought NBC's shares of Miss Universe, and then sold the entire company to the William Morris talent agency.

fired!" Throughout the first season, his portfolio got plenty of airtime as wannabe apprentices shilled Trump Ice and participated in challenges at Trump National Golf Club and Trump Taj Mahal in the hopes of winning the grand prize: a one-year job managing a Trump Organization project and a $250,000 salary.

Along the way, something else happened: America fell in love with the man who had once been a national punch line. Now, Trump was seen as a symbol of success and triumph, "whereas before, they viewed me as a bit of an ogre," he told *Esquire*. "People on the street embraced him," added Dowd. "All of a sudden, there was none of the old mocking. He was a hero." Trump was also warmly welcomed by Hollywood: For seven seasons, stars like Khloe Kardashian, Joan Rivers, Dennis Rodman and Geraldo Rivera clamored to align themselves with The Donald on *The Celebrity Apprentice*. And when his children Donald Jr., Ivanka and Eric

eventually joined their father in the boardroom, the Trump family was embraced as well—setting the stage for their next big move.

Ahead of the 15th season, Trump decided not to return as host (but would remain a producer). He had a far more important job to focus on: president of the United States. While campaigning, though, he caused controversy with his vow to build a wall on the U.S.-Mexico border. Amid backlash, NBC pulled *The Apprentice*, as well as the Miss Universe and Miss USA pageants, from its lineup. Trump sued the network for $500

million, but eventually settled for an undisclosed amount, as he looked ahead to the 2016 election.

And the rest is history: Trump's win signaled his segue from the boardroom to the Oval Office. Although the presidency spelled the end of his partnership with Burnett, their friendship remains—after all, the producer can be credited with elevating his national profile. Still, says *Apprentice* producer Katherine Walker, "I don't think any of us could have known what this would become. Donald would not be president had it not been for that show."

NO BUSINESS LIKE SHOW BUSINESS

Before Trump followed in his father's footsteps, he flirted with film school at the University of Southern California. "I was attracted to the glamour of the movies, and I admired guys like Sam Goldwyn, Darryl Zanuck and most of all Louis B. Mayer, whom I considered great showmen. But in the end I decided real estate was a much better business."

It was, and once he made a name for himself, Trump was drawn back to the glitz of Hollywood. His first cameo was in 1985 on *The Jeffersons*, and throughout the 1990s, he went on to play himself more than a dozen times on *The Fresh Prince of Bel-Air*, *The Nanny*, *Spin City* and *Sex and the City*—in addition to that famous 1995 Pizza Hut commercial with his ex-wife Ivana ("You're only entitled to half," he told her, as they negotiated the last slice). On the big screen, Trump has also had plenty of pop culture moments.

In 1996, he found a way to monetize his appreciation of beautiful women with the $10 million purchase of the Miss Universe Organization. The pageants, which aired first on CBS and then NBC, sold themselves, said Trump. "You don't have to spend money on sets. All you need is a beautiful curtain and the girls." Still, he turned around the televised shows that had been in "serious trouble." And in 2007, Trump was honored for the achievement—as well as his work as a co-producer on *The Apprentice*—with a star on the Hollywood Walk of Fame.

Trump was rivals with a billionaire developer (Hugh Grant) in *Two Weeks Notice*.

A STAR IS BORN
Trump's star on the Hollywood Walk of Fame is on a popular stretch of the boulevard near Britney Spears'.

LOVE & MARRIA

IVANA TRUMP AND "THE DONALD" HAD A LIFESTYLES OF THE RICH AND FAMOUS *MARRIAGE — UNTIL HE FELL FOR MARLA MAPLES.*

★ ★ ★ ★ ★

IN A CAMEO IN THE 1996 COMEDY *The First Wives Club*, Ivana Trump flashes a smile that's one part glamour, one part malevolence as she advises Diane Keaton, Goldie Hawn and Bette Midler how to get back at their exes. "Ladies, you have to be strong and independent," she says. "And remember—don't get mad, get everything!"

The first of Donald Trump's three wives was never one of his gilded playthings. A former Czech fashion model who could match her

husband zinger for zinger, Ivana was a tough businesswoman, a celebrity in her own right who knew her way around publicity and scandal, and a supporter of, but never an apologist for, her larger-than-life husband.

Married to Trump for 14 years, Ivana would be famously and scandalously replaced by a Hawaiian Tropic bikini model named Marla Maples who became wife No. 2 in 1993. She was a Georgia-bred beauty queen who on the surface seemed to share Ivana's blond good looks and

nothing else, but in fact embraced that most Trumpian of life codes: No apologies to anyone. "I never considered myself the mistress," Maples said recently to ABC News. "I mean, that's the truth."

Perhaps to her. To the New York tabloids (and, notably, to Ivana), Maples brought down not only a marriage but an institution, a pop culture icon—the power couple of all power couples.

When the first Mr. and Mrs. Trump ruled the Manhattan social scene

GE

STILL CONNECTED
Despite their bitter divorce, Ivana said in 2017 that she and Donald talk about once a week.

in the 1980s, "The Donald," as Ivana famously called him, referred to his wife as "my twin as a woman," perhaps the highest compliment a man of his boundless ego has ever bestowed upon another human being. She was also a woman who shared her husband's charisma and contradictions.

Born and raised in what was then called Czechoslovakia, Ivana Marie Zelníčková grew up with a love of skiing, marrying Austrian skier Alfred Winklmayr in 1971 and working as a model and ski instructor after they moved to Canada (they divorced two years later). Along the way, she had "somehow remained a woman of Old World East European values and sensibility," as *Vanity Fair* once said, an attitude that would serve her well when she met a tall, blond 29-year-old real estate man at Manhattan's tony Maxwell's Plum, where she was waiting to dine after a fashion show.

"He said, 'I'm Donald Trump and I see you're looking for a table. I can help you,'" Ivana recalled to the *New York Post* in 2016. "I look at my friends and said, 'The good news is, we're going to get a table real fast. The bad news is, this guy is going to be sitting with us.'"

Trump paid for the meal and left. "I said, 'There's something strange because I've never met a man who didn't want anything from a woman and paid for it,'" Ivana related.

After dating for less than a year, they married in 1977 in a lavish ceremony with 600 guests, of whom six were her friends. "I did not know anybody," she told ABC News. They had three children together—Donald Jr., Ivanka and Eric—and set about creating an empire, with Ivana quickly impressing her new husband with her insights into how to oversee the renovation of his first major Manhattan project, the Grand Hyatt. "I would send over one of my executives, or more often my wife, just to see how things were going," Trump said.

Next, she oversaw the design of his signature property, Trump Tower. "I picked out every piece of marble and every golden fixture in the place," she said. "The famous fountain in the lobby? My idea. The steel-and-glass facade? I pushed for that. I wanted the building that bore our name to be a modern marvel, to change the skyline of New York, and it did."

She was subsequently named president and CEO of the Trump Castle casino in Atlantic City. "I was tough but fair, and my employees loved me," she said. She then took on the renovation of The Plaza, famously working for $1 (she framed the check from her husband and hung it on her office wall). In 1988, Ivana became a naturalized U.S. citizen.

Each new project burnished the Trump brand and their fame, but privately their world was crumbling. As Donald teetered on the brink of personal bankruptcy with his

A SPECIAL PARTNERSHIP
The couple, here in 1982, worked together on his hotels and casinos. "I think Donald knew that I could achieve," Ivana said.

"DONALD WAS ALWAYS IN THE OFFICE... SO I HAD NO IDEA HOW HE HAD THE TIME TO CHEAT."

IVANA TRUMP, ON DONALD AND MARLA'S AFFAIR

In 1987, they had a photo shoot in their Greenwich, Connecticut, home. (Ivana got the house in the divorce.)

79

MOTHERHOOD, IVANA STYLE
Ivana, pictured in 1987 with Ivanka and Don Jr., would take the kids trick-or-treating with nannies and security guards.

The Original Helicopter Parent—With a Real Chopper

IVANA TRUMP RAISED HER CHILDREN WITH A FIRM HAND AND TIGHT BUDGET.

As Ivana Trump juggled parenting three children— Donald Jr., Ivanka and Eric—with her executive positions in the Trump real estate empire, she found the best solution was to take to the skies. "My version of helicopter parenting was to bring the kids to work with me in the Trump chopper," she wrote in her 2017 book, *Raising Trump.* "Why separate your two lives—career and family—if you can combine them?"

That meant a week for the children included a trip to Mom's "office," whether it be a boardroom or a construction site, to learn about business and life by example. When it came to money, though, the kids were expected to do as she said, not as she spent. "Keep them on a really low budget" is her advice for parenting rich kids.

After the Trumps' divorce, Ivana had sole custody of the children and made all the decisions from activities to education. Then, she said, "When each one finished college, I said to my ex-husband, 'Here is the finished product. Now it's your turn.'"

overextended investments in The Plaza and Atlantic City casinos, he began an affair with Marla, whom he'd met by bumping into her, literally, on Madison Avenue.

The troubles in the Trumps' marriage came to a head during a family vacation over Christmas 1989, when the 26-year-old Marla showed up at the same restaurant as 40-year-old Ivana. What happened next is in dispute. Ivana recalled an icy Marla telling her, "I'm Marla and I love your husband. Do you?" Ivana told TV host Barbara Walters that she responded, "Get lost. I love my husband very much." Other reports say Ivana called Marla a "bitch" and told her to leave her husband alone. Either way, the wounds never healed. "She actively participated in humiliating me in the media and indirectly put my kids at risk," Ivana wrote in 2017's *Raising Trump*.

The following February, Ivana got her revenge when she out-Donalded The Donald, dialing up *New York Daily News* gossip columnist Liz Smith while Trump was in Japan on business and spilling all. "Exclusive! Love on the Rocks," the paper's headline screamed, launching a string of stories. A vicious tabloid war ensued, with the rival *New York Post* countering with its own famous headline quoting Marla as saying: "Best sex I've ever had." The story was later revealed to have been planted by Donald.

"New York City is a very tough place," Ivana told *Vanity Fair*'s Marie

IN HINDSIGHT
Marla said she wished "more than anything" they'd dated after Donald divorced Ivana, as it would have saved a lot of "heartache."

Brenner. "I'm tough, too. When people give me a punch in the nose, I react by getting even tougher." She emerged victorious in the divorce, getting $14 million in cash, a 45-room mansion in Connecticut, custody of the three children and her dignity intact. Donald, in turn, got her silence: To this day, Ivana can't talk publicly about their marriage without his permission.

Both quickly realized that the public feuding was hurting the Trump brand, which could have a negative impact on future businesses ventures. "I wish Ivana the best," Donald said in a statement at the time of the divorce. "I have no doubt that she will do very well in the years to come." And Ivana did in fact go on to design lines of clothing, jewelry and beauty products and to write several books.

In 1993, a year after his divorce from Ivana, he proposed to Marla. Two months after welcoming daughter Tiffany in October 1993, they married at the Plaza Hotel with 1,000 guests in attendance including Rosie O'Donnell and O.J. Simpson.

EXTRAVAGANT WEDDING
Marla reportedly wore a $2 million diamond tiara at their December 1993 wedding at the Plaza Hotel in NYC.

DATING THE DONALD

ALONG WITH HIS THREE GLAMOROUS WIVES, TRUMP HAS STEPPED OUT WITH A STRING OF MODELS AND ACTRESSES.

Candice Bergen
In the 1960s while attending Wharton, Trump went on a date with the actress, who was then a Penn student. "He was a good-looking guy and a douche," Bergen later said on *Watch What Happens Live*.

Gabriela Sabatini
During a rumored break from then-mistress Marla Maples, Trump dated the tennis star for a month in 1989—she was only 19 while he was 43—before returning to Marla and divorcing Ivana.

Rowanne Brewer Lane
Spotting the model at a pool party in 1990, Trump reportedly said, "That's a stunning Trump girl right there." After their brief relationship, she married Jani Lane, front man of the band Warrant.

Kylie Bax
The New Zealand model dated Trump briefly in 1995 and later defended him against allegations of sexual harassment, suggesting some of his accusers were looking for "five minutes of fame."

Kara Young
After meeting at a party in the Hamptons in the late 1990s, Trump and the model-actress dated for two years. She went on to marry shipping billionaire Peter Georgiopoulos in 2005.

Allison Giannini
While separated from second wife Marla in 1997, Trump went on what would be a very bad blind date with the actress, who later said he only "talked about Marla and how much he loved her."

"I WANTED HIM TO SEE HOW LOVED HE COULD BE FOR HIS SOUL, NOT FOR HIS MONEY." MARLA MAPLES

HIS NEW FLAME
Marla, here with Donald in NYC early in their public relationship, called him "adorable... with a little-boy quality."

"The whole world was watching. He couldn't not wed the mother of his new baby, regardless of whether his heart was really in it," Ivana sniped in her 2017 book.

Marla played a lesser role in the Trump businesses, serving mostly as a face of the brand. She made guest-acting spots on shows like *Designing Women* and, with Donald, on *The Fresh Prince of Bel-Air*. She also appeared on Broadway in *The Will Rogers Follies* and co-hosted the Trump-owned Miss Universe pageant. They separated in 1997 and finalized their divorce in 1999, with Marla getting a settlement reported as being around $2 million. The reason for their split? "We differed on how we looked at the world and how we wanted to raise our child," she revealed in 2016.

And while their relationship played out as fodder for the media, Marla now believes a higher power was at work. "When Donald and I came together," she told ABC News, "I really felt that—I do believe there was divinity in it."

Although Ivana is now on friendly terms with Donald, she has never forgiven Marla, and in fact, won't even say her name. "That woman knowingly entered into a relationship with my husband, the father of three small children," Ivana wrote in her book. "The fact that the kids and I came through the entire ordeal stronger is irrelevant."

Marla Maples' Life After Divorce

THE MOTHER OF TRUMP'S DAUGHTER TIFFANY MOVED ON QUIETLY AND WITHOUT REMORSE, FOCUSING ON FAMILY, FAITH AND DANCING.

Raised a Southern Baptist, Marla Maples always appreciated the fact that her former husband, Donald Trump, would go with her to church. "It was really the biggest part of my life...wasn't the biggest part of his, I suppose," Maples, 56, said in 2018 on the Journeys of Faith With Paula Faris podcast. "You know, he's a man on a mission and always has been."

The mother of Donald's daughter Tiffany, 26, Marla and her presidential ex seem to have long ago put aside any animosity: Marla sat front-row at the inauguration and even posted an Instagram picture of herself waiting for her daughter to arrive.

Over the years, the former beauty queen and bikini model has appeared in the occasional movie, Broadway play and TV show, including *Dancing With the Stars* in 2016, where her tangos—on stage and with reporters, who only wanted to talk about her days with Trump—were offset by the joy of dancing. "This is the perfect medium to come back into the world and be myself," she told *The Hollywood Reporter*. "There's no time to be anything but yourself." While the woman she famously replaced continues to complain —"She's a showgirl. Never achieve anything in her life," said Ivana Trump in 2017—Marla instead focuses on faith and family.

"I just think life is about being ready for anything, you know, and where are you going to find the positive in all things," she said. "And I choose not to judge anybody else."

And sometimes life just dishes up its own revenge. Two years after she made fun of Marla for going on *Dancing With the Stars*, Ivana appeared on the Italian version of the show as a guest competitor.

STANDING TALL
Marla, a former *Dancing With the Stars* contestant, said she raised Tiffany in LA so she could "find her own identity."

★ ★ ★ ★ ★

WHEN DONALD MET
MELANIA

THE THIRD TIME WAS THE CHARM WHEN TRUMP WAS INTRODUCED TO THE
SLOVENIAN STUNNER WITH BRAINS THAT RIVAL HER EXOTIC BEAUTY.

"I was not starstruck," says Melania,
"and maybe he noticed that."

IN BUSINESS AND IN LIFE, DONALD
Trump is always up for a challenge.
One thing that often came easy,
though, was women—until he met
Melania Knauss. In 1998, a year
after he split from Marla Maples,
the 52-year-old was at a New York
Fashion Week party when his eyes
locked in on an exotic 5-foot-11
brunette who stood out in the
room full of models. Even though
he was there with a date, Donald
wondered to himself, "Who is that?"
He approached the mystery woman
with piercing eyes and pulled his
go-to move. "I tried to get her
number," Donald recalled, "and she
wouldn't give it to me." This time,

FAMILY MAN
Melania has said Donald possesses many of the same qualities as her father, Viktor: Both men are hardworking, smart and traditional.

ONE OF A KIND
Melania's custom wedding gown required 300 feet of material and more than 1,500 hours to create.

Model Moments

BEFORE SHE WAS MRS. DONALD TRUMP, MELANIA KNAUSS MADE A NAME FOR HERSELF IN EUROPE.

Melania's bridal *Vogue* cover wasn't the first time she graced the magazine. In her early modeling days, the brunette worked steadily in Milan and Paris, her photos filling the pages of the fashion bible's European editions. In 1996, she cashed in her savings to try the U.S. market. One of her first jobs: a Camel cigarettes ad for a billboard in Times Square.

After she started dating Trump, even more offers came in: Melania posed for famed photographers Helmut Newton and Mario Testino; scored the cover of *Ocean Drive*; and even appeared in *Sports Illustrated*'s swimsuit edition in 2000.

That same year, she covered *British GQ*—completely nude except for diamond jewelry aboard Donald's Boeing 727.

The racy mile high club–themed pictorial featured his lingerie-clad girlfriend posing in the cockpit and standing on a wing. The mogul was such a fan, he requested a framed cover be delivered to his office.

COVER GIRL 1 *GQ* was bombarded with requests to shoot Melania, and they delivered with "Sex at 30,000 ft." **2** In 1998, she worked a New York City runway in a bikini, accessorized with a dog.

"I DIDN'T KNOW MUCH ABOUT DONALD TRUMP. I HAD MY LIFE. I HAD MY WORLD."

MELANIA, WHEN SHE MET DONALD

his reputation preceded him, and 28-year-old Melania was no fool: "I had heard he was a ladies' man and so I said, 'I'm not one of the ladies.'"

Indeed, she wasn't. Born to a car dealer and fashion designer in a small town in Slovenia, Melania could speak five languages in addition to her native tongue (Serbo-Croatian, English, French, German and Italian) and studied architecture and design in college before dropping out to

model in Paris and Milan. During a scouting trip in Europe, she was discovered by ID Models founder Paolo Zampolli, who urged Melania to move to the United States. The Italian businessman went on to do more than help her fashion career— he was the one who introduced her to his good friend, Donald Trump.

Although most women would have jumped at the chance to date Manhattan's wealthiest playboy,

INSTANT ATTRACTION
"We had great chemistry," Melania said of their first meeting—although she waited weeks to call him.

MELANIA THROUGH THE YEARS

THE WOMAN WHO ONCE SAID THAT HER FAVORITE ITEM OF CLOTHING WAS JEANS HAS GROWN INTO HER ROLE AS THE WIFE OF A BILLIONAIRE BUSINESSMAN. OVER THE YEARS, HER STYLE HAS EVOLVED AS SHE'S GONE FROM CAREFREE MODEL TO SOCIETY MOM AND JEWELRY DESIGNER TO FIRST LADY OF THE UNITED STATES.

1987
Her first portfolio photo shoot came after a photographer saw the 17-year-old schoolgirl waiting for a friend.

2000
Trump's then-girlfriend made headlines in 2000 when she posed nearly nude for the cover of *British GQ* magazine.

Melania played it cool. Instead of giving Donald her number, she asked for his—and she paid close attention to which one he provided. "If he gave me just his office number, that would show he's not very serious," she explained. "It shows how a man sees a woman, and how he treats a woman." So how did Donald see Melania? He handed over the digits to his penthouse, office, jet, limo and Florida estate. Impressed, she still made him sweat it out. A week later, after a modeling gig in the Caribbean, Melania finally called. For their first date, Donald made reservations at the hottest club in the city, Moomba, and "we talked for almost the whole night," she remembers.

A month later, he whisked her off to Mar-a-Lago for the weekend aboard his private plane. Although

2002
As she settled into her life as Trump's significant other, her hairstyle and fashion choices became more sophisticated.

2017
Melania—whose Secret Service code name is Muse—knows that everything she wears as first lady makes a statement.

2018
She is a valuable asset to her husband on overseas trips, as she can speak as many as six languages.

TAKING CHARGE
Melania, with her husband at Mar-a-Lago in 1999, chose not to have a nanny for Barron, only employing a chef and an assistant.

Melania enjoyed the jet-set lifestyle that came with Donald, she was just as happy to enjoy a quiet night at home, a refreshing change from women he had been with in the past. Melania was certainly one of a kind—and she expected to be the only one.

Not long after they started dating, she broke it off with Donald. "She had some trust issues with him at the beginning," says her friend, photographer Matthew Atanian. "She was telling me that she wouldn't have it, he was back to his old ways. She kept her apartment to have her own space because of this." Within six months, the two were back together, and on the right path. Another two years later, she finally gave up her place to move into Donald's gilded Trump Tower penthouse. And in April 2004, he made it official when he proposed with a 12-carat diamond ring worth $2 million. "It was a great surprise," the future Mrs. Trump gushed to *The New York Post*. "We are very happy together."

The January 2005 wedding in Palm Beach was just as magical—and nearly televised for NBC (Melania nixed the idea). As celebrity guests including Heidi Klum, Simon Cowell, Barbara Walters and Kelly Ripa looked on, the bride walked down the aisle at the Episcopal Church of Bethesda-by-the-Sea in a custom-made Dior gown adorned with 1,500 crystal embellishments and trailed by a 13-foot train. Unlike at his wedding to Maples, Donald's three oldest children, plus Tiffany, were in attendance. The extravagant reception was held inside Mar-a-Lago's 17,000-square-foot ballroom, where they dined on beef tenderloin, caviar, lobster rolls and a 5-foot-tall Grand Marnier chocolate truffle cake, all washed down with Cristal Champagne—followed by Billy Joel serenading the newlyweds with "Just the Way You Are." The lavish affair was chronicled for a 17-page feature in *Vogue*, with "Donald Trump's New Bride" on the cover modeling her $200,000 gown and 16-foot veil.

Although Donald was nearing 60, starting a family was important to his new wife. "Melania would like to have children," he said. "I'm up for it." And they wasted no time: Barron was born in March 2006—and made Donald and Melania complete. She relished her new role as a mother, eschewing nannies and even her husband's help.

Inside Their Stunning Trump Tower Apartment

THE COUPLE'S THREE-STORY GILDED PALACE ON FIFTH AVENUE FEATURES A SEPARATE ELEVATOR AND PRIVATE WING FOR BARRON.

Gold, gold and more gold—the Trumps' three-story penthouse apartment gleams and glistens, from the crown molding accented with 24-karat gold to the lamps. Even the orange juice glasses are rimmed with gold! Accessible by a private elevator, the 10,996-square-foot space overlooking Central Park has been Donald's primary residence since Trump Tower went up in 1983, though it has gotten even more opulent since then.

Chandeliers illuminate plush furnishings in Louis XIV-style, including candelabras and bronze statues, while portraits of family members hang on the walls along with a painting of the Greek sun god Apollo led in his chariot by the dawn goddess, Aurora. Behind the sitting room, a fountain gurgles and the family crest decorates throw pillows. Melania has a separate business office and son Barron has an entire floor to himself where he grew up building Lego airports. In 2017, the Manhattan apartment, which Trump says has "the Tiffany location" because it means the best, was valued at $64 million by *Forbes*.

"BETWEEN ME AND MY HUSBAND, I KNOW EVERYTHING THAT IS GOING ON." MELANIA TRUMP

When Donald came home after a long day at Trump Organization, "I didn't want him to change the diapers or put Barron to bed."

Melania has been so hands-on with her son, she put her own business aspirations, like her jewelry line (see below for more), on the back burner until he started school. "I am a full-time mom; that is my first job," she told *Parenting*. "The most important job ever. When he is in school I do my meetings, my sketches and everything else." As fulfilling as motherhood has been for Melania, she doesn't envision giving Barron a younger sibling. "I don't like to say never, but my life is very busy," she told *ABC News*. "We are happy and my hands are full with my two boys —my big boy and my little boy!"

As she and Donald celebrate more than two decades together, Melania has made it further than either of the two wives before her. What's her secret? Besides separate bathrooms, their differing temperaments help to keep the balance. "When he is spinning and thinking and blazing forward, she brings this quality of calm and serenity to him," explains Melania's friend, CNN producer Pamela Gross. And in return, Donald spoils his better half with more than just material gifts (for their 10th wedding anniversary, she received a 25-carat diamond ring). "If I say, 'I need an hour, I'm going to take a bath,' or I'm having a massage, he [has] nothing against it. He's very supportive in that way," Melania's said.

The couple also thrive on mutual respect and their individuality. "I give him my opinions, and sometimes he takes them in, and sometimes he does not. Do I agree with him all the time? No. I think it is good for a healthy relationship. I am not a 'yes' person. No matter who you are married to, you still need to lead your life. I don't want to change him. And he doesn't want to change me."

SHE'S A BUSINESSWOMAN, TOO

Being married to The Donald has rubbed off. In 2010, Mrs. Trump launched Melania Jewelry & Timepieces, selling out in 45 minutes during its QVC debut. The three collections, priced from $30 to $200, each represented the charm of her favorite cities: NYC (business), Palm Beach (sporty) and Paris (sparkly), with versatility to wear from day to night.

Melania also created a short-lived skin-care line of facial lotions, exfoliators and cleansers infused with anti-aging caviar available at Lord & Taylor department stores. Unfortunately, before business even took off it was torpedoed by its investment company, whose founders had a legal falling out.

Although Melania shuttered her business when she became first lady, after the White House, she could very well resurrect her brand. "I studied design so I have many, many ideas for home, for clothing," she revealed to Fox Business. "I love beauty and fashion, so we will see in the future."

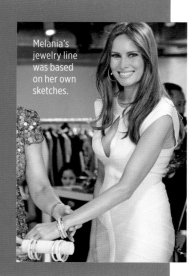

Melania's jewelry line was based on her own sketches.

THE LIGHT OF HER LIFE
Melania is a very hands-on parent with her son, Barron, calling motherhood the "most important job ever."

PROUD DAD
"My children really like me—love me—a lot," Trump says of his five kids. "They're very grounded and very solid."

NEXT GEN

THE PRESIDENT SAYS THE HARDEST THING ABOUT RAISING KIDS WAS FINDING

ERATION

TIME TO SPEND WITH THEM, BUT THEY'RE NOW CHIPS OFF THE OLD BLOCK.

RUNNING FOR OFFICE?
"I never want to rule it out," Donald Jr. said about moving into politics. "I definitely enjoy the fight."

DONALD JR.
OUT OF HIS DAD'S SHADOW

THE ELDEST TRUMP CHILD OVERCOMES FAMILY PRESSURES TO BECOME HIS FATHER'S BIGGEST ALLY — AND WEAPON.

At 6, he played in his father's office while Donald made deals.

HE DRAWS CROWDS OF
thousands for speeches and rallies. He's a top-requested speaker for television appearances. He can match and often exceed his father's ferocity on social media. He keeps the base energized.

That Donald Trump Jr. would emerge as his father's secret weapon speaks to how far he has come in a life journey that by his own reckoning has been a bumpy one from even before he was born, starting with his mother, Ivana, pressing for him to be named after his father. "You can't do that!" Donald, then 31, reportedly shouted. "What if he's a loser?"

He grew up in the palatial penthouse at the top of Trump Tower in New York, watched over by nannies and bodyguards. Later Donald Jr. attended boarding school and spent summers with his maternal grandparents in Czechoslovakia, where he developed

Donald and his ex-wife, Vanessa, vowed to make sure their kids were always a top priority.

BLOND BEAUTY
Before marrying Donald Jr., Vanessa, who was born and raised in NYC, was a Wilhelmina model who dated Leonardo DiCaprio.

After graduating from his father's alma mater, Wharton School of the University of Pennsylvania, he departed for Aspen, Colorado, where he hunted, fished, bartended—and, he admits, drank too much, according to *New York*—a lifestyle that followed him back to the Big Apple before he gave it up. "I have too much of an opportunity to make something of myself, be successful in my own right," he told the magazine. "Why blow it?"

He began dating model-socialite Vanessa Haydon after his father pointed out the pretty blonde to him at a party. They wed at a lavish ceremony at Mar-a-Lago in 2005, had five children—Kai, Donald Trump III, Tristan, Spencer, and Chloe—and he dedicated himself to the Trump business, even appearing on *The Apprentice*. After serving a high-profile role in the presidential campaign, Donald Jr. now runs the Trump Organization with younger brother Eric, and still faces those Trumpian pressures: He went through his own headline-making 2018 divorce and high-profile new relationship with Fox News personality Kimberly Guilfoyle.

Only now he's a Trump on his own terms. "It is not just that he is trying to help his father," longtime friend Tom Hicks Jr. told the *Los Angeles Times*. "He has a real passion for the ideas." And he's recording those ideas on paper: His book, *Triggered: How the Left Thrives on Hate and Wants to Silence Us*, was released in 2019.

a lifelong love of the outdoors and coped with his dad's absences. "It wasn't a 'Hey, son, let's go play catch in the backyard' kind of father-son relationship," he told the *Washington Post*. "It was, 'Hey, you're back from school? Come down to the office.'"

It was Donald Jr. who bore the toughest burden when his parents divorced. He was only 12 when his mother told him about his father's affair with Marla Maples. "You don't love us! You don't even love yourself. You just love your money!" he yelled at his father, according to *Vanity Fair*, and for a year, Donald Jr. didn't talk to his father and refused his phone calls.

"I'M SUCH A DIFFERENT PERSON, IT'S HARD TO EVEN COMPARE US."

DONALD JR., ON BEING LIKENED TO HIS DAD

"I always have my heart open and my calendar available," Kimberly Guilfoyle said about possibly marrying Don Jr.

MRS. PRESIDENT?

"If she ever wanted to run for president, I think she'd be very, very hard to beat," Donald told *The Atlantic* of Ivanka.

IVANKA
HER FATHER'S FAVORITE

TRUMP'S ELDEST DAUGHTER FINDS HER OWN VOICE — EVEN IF IT CLASHES WITH HER DAD'S.

WHEN MOM AND DAD NIXED A lemonade stand in front of Trump Tower, Ivanka Trump and her brothers set up shop at the family's Connecticut summer home—a buzzkill for business, as the mansion sat at the end of a cul-de-sac in a neighborhood where butlers bring the beverages.

So using what Ivanka called their "wily charms and persuasive marketing skills," they convinced the only customers around—bodyguards, chauffeur and maids—to dig out their spare change. "We made the best of a bad situation, I guess—a lesson we'd utilize again and again as we moved on in business," Ivanka wrote in her 2009 book, *The Trump Card*.

For a Trump, when life gives you lemons, make money. Try as her parents did to instill traditional values, Ivanka had to absorb them in the most nontraditional of circumstances. It meant she became a Trump—tough, driven, competitive—but also uniquely herself.

Since her father's election, Ivanka, whose title is assistant to the president, has been called a stabilizing force, "the quiet power behind Trump," according to Politico. Ivanka looks at her role

DADDY'S GIRL
About her childhood, Ivanka has said, "I really appreciated having a set of traditions."

Ivanka, with her mother in 1987, is called "Baby" by her doting dad.

"WE WERE SORT OF BRED TO BE COMPETITIVE." IVANKA TRUMP

as her father's adviser from another angle. "I'm his daughter. I've known him my entire life. He trusts me," she told *The New York Times*. "I don't have a hidden agenda. I'm not looking to hit him to help myself."

From the moment Ivana Marie Trump (the "Ivanka" is a diminutive of her first name) was born in 1981, family and the family business were inseparable, and it wasn't always easy. As a young child, she recalls,

her father—then building a real estate empire—was somebody both close and distant.

"He wasn't always physically present," she says, "but he was always available," usually by phone whenever she needed him. Her parents went out every night, but not before a dinner at home, followed by a bath for Ivanka and 45 minutes in her pajamas talking to her mother, Ivana, as she glammed up for an evening on the town.

ALWAYS WORKING
In her 2017 book, Ivanka said, "Learning to negotiate is essential to truly staking your claim."

Her parents tried to shield her from the worst of the attention, but she was never immune. "There were definitely times when I was younger I was going, 'Did you have to say that, Dad?'" she told Oprah Winfrey. Nor did she escape, at a tender age, the fallout from her father's affair with Marla Maples and her parents' high-profile divorce when she was 10. A reporter once shouted to little Ivanka, "Is it true that Marla said that your father was the best sex she ever had?"

Otherwise, life was as normal as it could be for the daughter of a flashy billionaire. Through age 15, Ivanka attended an upper-crust private school in Manhattan, then was sent to boarding school at Choate Rosemary Hall in Connecticut. She went through a mild rebellious period, her "punk phase in the '90s," she calls it, when she listened to Nirvana records, wore ripped jeans and flannel shirts, and dyed her hair blue (her mother forced her to dye it back to blond herself with a $10 box of Nice'n Easy).

Tall and beautiful, Ivanka began modeling in her teens, gracing the cover of *Seventeen*'s issue on celebrity moms and daughters in 1997 and walking the catwalk for Versace and Thierry Mugler. But business was her main calling. She followed her father to construction sites, learned to read architectural renderings and sat quietly in her mother's office while she met with contractors and worked deals. "Mom allowed us to flourish and learn from watching her, listening to her conversations, and seeing how she handled herself," she wrote in her mother's memoir, *Raising Trump*.

"I always envisioned myself having a traditional and elegant wedding," Ivanka has said.

Like her older brother, she graduated from her father's alma mater, Wharton School of the University of Pennsylvania, with a bachelor's degree in economics in 2004, and the following year, at only 24, Ivanka joined The Trump Organization as a vice president in charge of development and acquisitions, while pursuing her own business ventures, including lines of jewelry, shoes and handbags. She also wrote two books and appeared on her father's reality show, *The Apprentice*, where she evaluated contestants in tense boardroom moments.

In 2009, she married real estate developer Jared Kushner in a Jewish ceremony (she converted), two years after they met at a business lunch. "He's incredibly relaxed and calm. The world could be collapsing around him, and nothing fazes him. He's very solution-oriented," she told *Vogue*. "Plus it was nice finding someone who is a genuinely good person."

The pair share three children—Arabella, Joseph, and Theodore—and Ivanka admits that she carefully schedules her days to ensure she gets to spend quality time with her family. "Being a mother is the most rewarding experience, but also the most wild and stressful," she admitted in 2016.

In an essay for *Business Insider* that same year, Ivanka explained that her parenting skills made her a better businesswoman. "You can't instruct your children to respect people and have good manners if you yourself don't say 'please' and 'thank you.' As a leader, you also set the tone," she wrote. "You must be willing to work the hardest in the room; you cannot expect your team to meet—and surpass—high expectations if you don't hold yourself to that same standard."

FAMILY BUSINESS
Lara, a former producer for *Inside Edition,* is a senior adviser to her father-in-law's reelection campaign, often speaking at rallies.

Like his big brother, Eric is into outdoor pursuits like hunting.

ERIC
"TEDDY BEAR" WITH A GROWL

THE YOUNGEST OF DONALD'S THREE CHILDREN WITH IVANA LIVES UP TO — AND DASHES — EXPECTATIONS AS HE RUNS THE TRUMP BUSINESS.

AT A TOWERING 6-FOOT-5, ERIC Trump stands out in a crowd, as he did one day when he caught the eye of television producer Lara Yunaska in New York. Herself an inch shy of 6 feet in stocking feet, Lara recalled they were "probably the two tallest people in the room," and she was immediately intrigued.

On their first date, Lara kept her expectations in check. "I was like: This guy must be sort of what you would expect from a rich guy's son," she recalled to the *Star News* of Wilmington, North Carolina. "But it ended up being the best date I've ever been on."

The youngest of Donald Trump's three children with first wife Ivana, Eric has spent a lifetime confronting and dashing the outsize expectations that come with his surname. Certainly that was true for Lara—they married in 2014, welcomed son Eric Jr. three years later, and daughter Carolina in 2019—and it continues to be so for others. "Eric is extremely warm and friendly, a big wide-open smile, handshake," *60 Minutes'* Lesley Stahl told *Vanity Fair.* "He comes across as a teddy bear."

Eric's childhood played out in the tabloid glare of his parents' spectacular divorce. With custody of the children granted to their Ivana, Eric and Donald Jr. spent

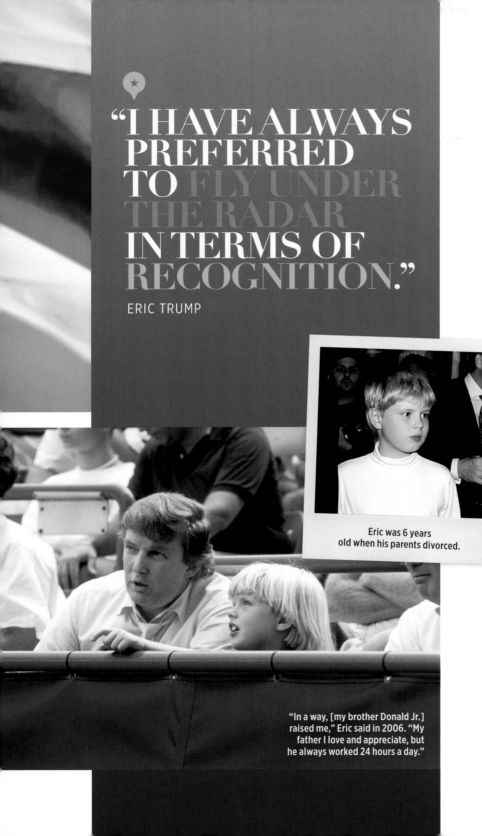

"I HAVE ALWAYS PREFERRED TO FLY UNDER THE RADAR IN TERMS OF RECOGNITION."

ERIC TRUMP

Eric was 6 years old when his parents divorced.

"In a way, [my brother Donald Jr.] raised me," Eric said in 2006. "My father I love and appreciate, but he always worked 24 hours a day."

much of their time with their mother and her parents, with summers abroad in Ivana's native Czechoslovakia.

Father Donald remained a powerful, if physically distant, force in his life, and Eric now channels some of Dad's outspokenness on his Twitter page. This bear can growl! After Eric graduated from Georgetown University in 2006, he went into the family business as an executive and appeared on *The Apprentice* before serving as a presidential campaign adviser. Now running the Trump empire with Don Jr., Eric remains a Trump, but one with his own style.

In 2011, he was appointed president of his father's newly acquired 227-acre winery in Charlottesville, Virginia, and two years later was named *Wine Enthusiast*'s Rising Star of the Year. Eric now owns the business, with the Trump Winery's sparkling, red and white wines winning awards. "It's so much fun to be able to take our knowledge of development and apply it to a little bit of a different arena and we've been amazingly successful," he said in 2016. "It's been a great business, a very different business. It's a very sexy business."

"Eric has Trump genes, but he doesn't have the Trump brand," college classmate and friend Clare Fieseler told the *Washington Post*. "I've always admired that he is uniquely his own in that way. Less bombastic, more thoughtful. Less self-aggrandizing, more humble. Less Trump. More Eric."

TIFFANY
ASPIRING POP STAR TURNED LEGAL SCHOLAR

THE PRESIDENT'S YOUNGEST DAUGHTER KEEPS A LOW PROFILE IN POLITICS, BUT SHINES ON SOCIAL MEDIA—AND IN LAW SCHOOL.

A CLOSE BOND
"My friends and everyone I know are like, 'Wow, you guys really have a good relationship,'" Tiffany said of her mom, Marla.

Tiffany was able to enjoy her childhood away from public scrutiny.

IF DONALD TRUMP IS THE TWITTER president, then Tiffany Trump is the Snapchat first daughter. She receives less attention than her older half-siblings, Donald Jr., Ivanka and Eric. She largely stayed off the campaign trail to focus on her studies at the University of Pennsylvania and makes few appearances at the White House while pursuing her law degree at Georgetown. But on social media, she's a star, posting for her 1 million Instagram followers a stream of pouty glamour shots, bikini pics, family photos with her dad and stepmom, Melania, and scenes of her jet-setting lifestyle from Cannes to New York, as well as loving portraits with Marla Maples, who raised her as a single mother.

Born in 1993 in West Palm Beach, Florida, Tiffany got her name from the famous Fifth Avenue jewelry store next to Trump Tower. "We have a perfect little girl, a combination in looks of both of us, to go with my three other wonderful children," Trump told *The New York Times* 20 minutes after her birth, though he later infamously told Howard Stern that her arrival was unplanned.

Tiffany was just 6 years old when her parents divorced in 1999 after a six-year marriage overshadowed by Marla's scandal-making affair with Trump while he was still married to first wife Ivana. After her

While all the Trump children have spoken candidly of their father's hands-off parenting approach, Tiffany was particularly cut off. She saw her father and half-siblings during spring break trips to Mar-a-Lago and sometimes at Trump Tower, where she even had to seek Ivanka's advice on how to handle negotiations with the ultimate dealmaker to get a higher allowance.

"Big Sis did an end-around to save Tiffany the trouble," Ivanka recalled in her book *The Trump Card*. "I didn't tell her, of course, but I went to our father and suggested he think about surprising Tiffany with a credit card for Christmas, with a small monthly allowance on it. Sure enough, he did just that. Tiffany was thrilled and relieved. And appreciative."

Apart from a brief dalliance with pop stardom, when she released the single "Like a Bird" at the age of 17, Tiffany has kept a low profile, although she made a rare speaking appearance during the 2016 presidential campaign at the Republican National Convention. She has a circle of rich and famous friends given the name the Snap Pack for their many social media posts, including pics with her boyfriend, businessman Michael Boulos.

But one post stands out: an August 2016 photo of a stack of law school admission test study guides with the caption, "I got this."

Soon after, she was accepted to Georgetown's law school.

"I HAVE A STRONG HEAD ON MY SHOULDERS."

TIFFANY TRUMP

divorce, Marla moved her daughter to California and settled outside Los Angeles, where Tiffany grew up largely out of the public eye compared to her half-siblings who stayed in New York. Tiffany was spared the publicity and scrutiny that came with being a Trump, for which her mother is grateful. "I had the blessing of raising her pretty much on my own," Marla told *The New York Times*.

"I'm definitely different from all of them growing up on the East Coast," Tiffany told Oprah Winfrey about her siblings in 2013. "It was great for me getting to grow up as a normal kid just out of the spotlight, versus all of them growing up in New York. They always had that intense spotlight on them."

FUN IN THE SUN
At Mar-a-Lago, Barron and his dad "play golf, spend time together, eat together" and "enjoy family time," Melania says.

Barron is bilingual and speaks fluent Slovenian.

BARRON
"LITTLE DONALD"

THE FAMILY KEEPS THE PRESIDENT'S YOUNGEST SON OUT OF THE PUBLIC EYE, BUT HE SHOWS TRUMPIAN TRAITS.

AT THE FINALE PARTY FOR *The Celebrity Apprentice* in 2015, Barron Trump, almost 9, wore a black suit that matched the one worn by his father. "Sometimes I call him Little Donald," mom Melania told parenting.com in 2012, and the similarities don't end with the coordinated wardrobe. "He is independent and opinionated and knows exactly what he wants."

As the president's youngest child has moved from New York to the White House—the first time a presidential son has lived there since the Kennedy era—add one more parallel to Dad: A growth spurt at age 13 puts him over 6 feet tall.

While half-siblings Donald Jr., Ivanka, Eric and Tiffany have spoken of the challenges of growing up Trump, Barron appears to be the most shielded of the clan, benefiting from being the baby of the family.

Born on March 20, 2006, to Donald's third wife, Barron grew up on his own floor in Trump Tower, where he was allowed to scribble with crayons on his playroom walls (they were repeatedly painted over), and he

attended his dad's elementary school alma mater, the Columbia Grammar and Preparatory School. Melania has always been his primary caregiver. Trump, who was 59 when Barron was born, once told Howard Stern, "She takes care of the baby and I pay all of the costs!" For her part, Melania was "completely fine with that," adding, "Children need your attention, they need to see that you are involved and they really want their mommy there."

After his father moved into the White House in early 2017, Barron stayed behind in New York with

"HE IS A VERY STRONG-MINDED, VERY SPECIAL, SMART BOY." MELANIA TRUMP

Melania to finish the school year, and then transferred to St. Andrew's Episcopal School, a college-prep school in Potomac, Maryland. That made him the first presidential child in more than 35 years to not attend Sidwell Friends.

During his father's presidency, Barron splits his time in Washington between his private school and playing soccer at D.C. United's Development Academy. Like his father, Barron "is a good athlete," Trump says. "He loves soccer."

That Barron is seldom seen in public gives him more in common with his half-sibling Tiffany (though she is on Instagram) than with the other Trump kids. One rare Barron photo op came at the annual White House Easter Egg Roll in 2018, but he stayed back with his parents while his younger nieces and nephews searched for eggs. Another was when he strolled across the tarmac with his parents over Thanksgiving 2018.

But make no mistake: Barron is very much a Trump. As a child, he played for hours with his Lego bricks and Magna-Tiles, imagining airports and entire cities. Said Melania: "He builds big projects."

ROLE MODEL
"I teach him what is right, what is wrong," Melania said. "He doesn't have social media yet, he's not interested in it. He's all into sports."

Barron's protective mom works hard to shield her son from invasions of privacy.

DONALD TRUMP

111

THE GOP'S CHOICE
"We will lead our party back to the White House," Trump told the RNC when he was nominated.

TRUMP FOR PRESIDENT

★ ★ ★ ★ ★

AFTER YEARS OF CRITICIZING U.S. POLITICS, THE BILLIONAIRE PUT HIS MONEY WHERE HIS MOUTH WAS AND LAUNCHED A PRESIDENTIAL CAMPAIGN THAT DEFIED ALL EXPECTATIONS.

THROUGHOUT HIS SUCCESSFUL business career, the prospect of Donald Trump running for president came up repeatedly. It was certainly an idea he toyed with: First in 1987 when he proclaimed, "I believe that if I did run for president, I'd win," followed by brief considerations in the 2000, 2004 and 2012 elections. But after Barack Obama was elected to a second term, Trump couldn't remain silent—and he decided it was time to do something about it.

"Everybody tells me, 'Please run for president. Please run for president,'" he told a crowd of thousands at a Republican event in Michigan in May 2013. "I would be much happier if a great and competent person came along. I'd be happy if President Obama did a great job. I'm a Republican, but before anything, I love this country. I would love to see somebody come in who is going to be great." In that same speech, Trump predicted Obama's Secretary of State Hillary Clinton would be the Democratic nominee in the 2016 election— and if the GOP didn't "pick the right person, it will be a landslide" victory for her.

But was he the man for the job? Before Trump could make a decision, he needed to be sure. A true strategist, he commissioned electoral research, spending $1 million to determine his standing in each of America's 50 states and gauge how many voters he'd effectively need

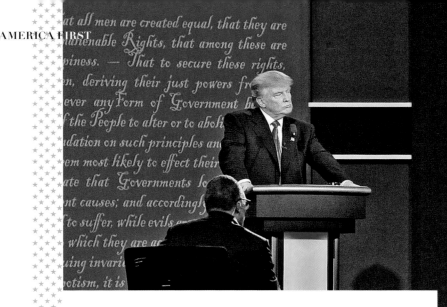

Most-Watched Debate in TV History

THE FIRST TIME DONALD TRUMP AND HILLARY CLINTON SQUARED OFF, A RECORD NUMBER TUNED IN.

With *The Apprentice*, Trump was used to commanding a television audience—but his first debate with Hillary Clinton pulled in more than four times the number of viewers. According to Nielsen, the September 26, 2016, event drew a record-breaking 84 million people across 13 channels, in addition to 8 million views (not unique viewers) on Facebook; another 3.4 million streamed it on YouTube and CBS All Access, making it the most-watched presidential debate in television history.

The previous record was held by incumbent Jimmy Carter and Ronald Reagan for their lone debate in 1980, with 80.6 million viewers. (In comparison, Barack Obama and Mitt Romney only pulled in 67 million.) Even more impressive about Trump and Clinton's first showdown was that viewership remained high throughout their 98-minute debate, with very little drop-off after the first half hour.

Although Clinton was deemed the winner by the mainstream media, social media said otherwise. On Twitter, 62 percent favored Trump during the "most tweeted debate ever," while on Facebook he controlled a whopping 79 percent of the conversation across the platform.

"IT'S A LONG ROAD. MY HUSBAND HAS A LOT OF PEOPLE CHEERING FOR HIM. WE WILL SEE."

MELANIA TRUMP

to win over. The results must have been promising, because on June 16, 2015, the real estate magnate formally announced his presidential campaign from the lobby of Trump Tower in New York City.

Surrounded by a throng of press, cheering supporters waving signs, and his adoring family, Trump descended the escalator to Neil Young's "Rockin' in the Free World." As he took to a podium bearing his name, thousands of fans peered down from the atrium's five stories to hear him speak. Flanked by eight American flags, the Republican candidate—dressed in a red tie, white shirt and blue suit, no less—spent 45 minutes carefully

laying out his plan to Make America Great Again: He'd repeal Obamacare, save Social Security, end illegal immigration, strengthen the military, protect the Second Amendment and, as a billion-dollar businessman, renegotiate disadvantageous foreign trade deals. "Our country needs a truly great leader," he told the crowd amid chants of "We want Trump." "And we need a truly great leader now.... Sadly, the American dream is dead. But if I get elected president, I will bring it back, bigger and better and stronger than ever before—and we will make America great again."

Reactions were mixed: Some supported Trump's bid for the White

House, others thought it was a joke, but most didn't think he had a snowball's chance in hell. Once he hit the campaign trail, though, aboard his private Boeing 757 Trump Force One, doubters were made believers—or at the very least, he had their full attention. A politician with little regard for political correctness, Trump was a breath of fresh air to many Americans. And as he stumped all over the country, from primary states Iowa and New Hampshire to Democratic-stronghold cities like Las Vegas and Los Angeles, he quickly gained traction.

Within weeks, Trump became the front-runner of the 17 GOP

"WE WILL FACE CHALLENGES. WE WILL CONFRONT HARDSHIPS. BUT WE WILL GET THE JOB DONE."

PRESIDENT DONALD TRUMP, IN HIS INAUGURATION SPEECH

First lady Melania, President Trump and first daughter Tiffany greet supporters at his January 2017 inauguration.

TRUMP WINS US PRESIDENCY

President-elect Donald Trump lived up to his boisterous campaign rhetoric, pulling off a come-from-behind to win the 270 Electoral College votes he needed for victory.

Hillary Clinton Tim Kaine — **218** (47.2%)

ELECTORAL COLLEGE VOTES NEEDED TO WIN PRESIDENCY — **270**

Donald Trump Mike Pence — **274** (48%)

■ DEMOCRATIC WIN ■ REPUBLICAN WIN ■ LIKELY DEMOCRATIC WIN ■ LIKELY REPUBLICAN WIN

"THAT MAP WAS BLEEDING RED"

ON ELECTION NIGHT, NO ONE TRULY KNEW WHAT TO EXPECT — MOST OF ALL DONALD TRUMP.

candidates, including former Florida Governor Jeb Bush. With the reality star nipping at their heels, many took shots at him. "I think in terms of a commander-in-chief," said Texas Senator Ted Cruz, "we ought to have someone who isn't springing out of bed to tweet in a frantic response to the latest polls."

The first primary proved his opponents wouldn't go down without a fight. Ahead of the Iowa caucus in February 2016, the campaign of his closest rival, Cruz, falsely implied in an email that Ben Carson was quitting the race and encouraged the neurosurgeon turned politician's supporters to cast their vote for Cruz instead. They did, and the Texan beat out Trump, who immediately cried fraud.

"Ted Cruz didn't win Iowa, he stole it," Trump tweeted. But in Cruz, he found his match. "Yet another #Trumpertantrum," the

Until Trump was officially named the winner, it was a roller coaster of emotions, which he recounted for supporters during a victory tour stop in West Allis, Wisconsin, on December 13, 2016. "Should I go over that evening just once quickly?" the president-elect teased.

"So it began with phony exit polls," explained Trump, who received a phone call from his daughter Ivanka and her husband, Jared Kushner, at 5 p.m. "They said, 'I'm sorry, Dad. It looks really bad. Looks really, really bad.'" Trump was so convinced, he reached

out to running mate Mike Pence to tell him, "It's not looking good." Next, he turned to his wife, Melania. "Baby, I'll tell you what, we're not gonna win tonight because the polls have come out.... It's just looking bad. But, you know what, I'm OK with it, because of the fact that I couldn't have worked any harder."

But Melania had faith in her husband. She was confident he'd pull out the win—and he hoped she was right, as he fretted about giving his concession speech in the small ballroom he had rented out for the night. Why not a big ballroom? "Because I didn't know if I was gonna win or lose," Trump admitted. But then the polls closed and "the real numbers started coming."

In a mock newscaster voice, he delivered the "breaking news": Trump had won in Ohio, Iowa,

Florida, North Carolina, Michigan, Wisconsin and Pennsylvania, as well as traditionally Republican states that polls suggested Clinton could steal: Arizona, Georgia and Utah. "Then it happened, folks, out of nowhere," said Trump. "Boy, that map was getting red as hell. That map—that map was bleeding red. That map was so beautiful-looking. And I'll never forget the guy who was saying for months: 'There is no path to 270 [electoral college votes] for Donald Trump.' But there was a path to 306.

"I'll never forget when they were on the map and they put up Wisconsin, and he said, 'There is no path for Hillary Clinton to become president,'" Trump concluded, sparking a deafening roar from the crowd. "'Donald Trump is your next president of the United States.'"

117

senator replied on Twitter. By the New Hampshire primary, though, Trump bounced back in magnificent fashion: He received 35 percent of the vote, the biggest victory in the state's Republican primary since 2000.

After more triumphs—in South Carolina, Nevada, Indiana and four other key states—Trump was declared the winner of Super Tuesday on March 1. By this point, it was clear the Republican fight for the White House was only his to lose, and within two months, all remaining GOP hopefuls dropped out of the race. The last man standing, Trump was crowned the presumptive Republican nominee, set to battle it out in the general election against the Democrat he had predicted just a year earlier. In an interview with *Time* magazine, he showed no fear of Clinton: "I am the last person on Earth she wants to run against."

And he immediately proved why. In his acceptance speech at the Republican National Convention, Trump evoked Clinton's name 11 times, as he called out her subpar record during her tenure as Obama's secretary of state. "America is far less safe—and the world is far less stable— than when Obama made the decision to put Hillary Clinton in charge of America's foreign policy," said Trump. "In 2009, pre-Hillary, ISIS was not even on the map." On her watch, he noted, ISIS had spread, Iraq was in chaos, Iran was destined for nuclear weapons, and Syria was engulfed in a civil war leading to a refugee crisis. "After 15 years of wars in the Middle East, after trillions of dollars spent and thousands of lives lost, the situation is worse than it has ever been before.

SENSE OF HUMOR
When one of the babies he held at a Colorado rally in July 2016 began to wail, Trump joked, "Don't worry...I hear that baby crying, I like it."

A WINNER
"I'm the most successful person ever to run for the presidency, by far," Trump told *The Des Moines Register* before launching his campaign.

"We Are Going to Make Our Country Great Again"

By launching his presidential campaign from his gilded 58-story Manhattan skyscraper, Trump sent a message—he would be bringing his talents as a businessman to the table.

Wearing a blue suit, red tie and white shirt that echoed the colors of the American flags behind him, Trump announced his run for the presidency in June 2015 with a 45-minute speech, laying out his plan to Make America Great Again. Pointing out his $8.7 billion net worth, he said his wealth and successful career not only qualified him to "be the greatest jobs president that God ever created," but it would allow him to self-fund his campaign and avoid the pressures of lobbyists and special-interest groups.

Trump promised he would repeal Obamacare, make Mexico pay for a wall on the southern border and be tougher on ISIS than anyone else. He also stated he'd renegotiate trade deals that he said left America looking like a third-world country.

"Our enemies are getting stronger and stronger by the day, and the U.S. as a country is getting weaker and weaker," he told the crowd. "How stupid are our leaders, how stupid are our politicians to let this happen?

"Our country needs a truly great leader," Trump added. "And we need a truly great leader now. We need a leader that wrote *The Art of the Deal*, we need a leader that can bring back our jobs, can bring back our manufacturing, can bring back our military and take care of our vets."

"IT IS TIME FOR US TO COME TOGETHER AS ONE UNITED PEOPLE."

PRESIDENT TRUMP, IN HIS VICTORY SPEECH

This is the legacy of Hillary Clinton: death, destruction and weakness. But Hillary Clinton's legacy does not have to be America's legacy."

Early in the race, Clinton seemed a lock to become the 45th president. But just months ahead of election night, Trump was quickly closing in on her once-significant lead, following the FBI's investigation into her use of her personal email to conduct official (and highly classified) business. There were bumps on the road for Trump, too: Ahead of the second debate, controversy erupted with the leak

SIGNS OF SUCCESS
Several of Trump's rallies in 2015 and 2016 attracted crowds of more than 20,000 people.

of a 2005 *Access Hollywood* tape in which Trump can be heard making lewd comments about women. He apologized profusely, but refused to let it end his bid for the presidency. "The media and establishment want me out of the race so badly," he tweeted.

Trump also fought fire with fire: Two hours before the debate, he held a press conference with three women who had accused Bill Clinton of inappropriate sexual behavior in the past. "I'm here to support Mr. Trump because he's going to make America great again," said Paula Jones, a former Arkansas state employee who famously sued the president in 1994 for sexual harassment. "I think they should all look at the fact that he's a good person and he's not what other people say he's being, like Hillary." If that wasn't enough to make his opponent squirm, Trump invited the women to that evening's televised debate in St. Louis, also attended by Hillary's husband.

In the end, the American people had the last word—and it was Trump. On November 8, 2016, in a stunning upset, he was elected president with 304 electoral votes, despite Clinton winning the popular vote by 2.9 million. In his victory speech Trump began by recognizing his opponent's "very, very hard-fought campaign" and giving credit where it was due, telling the crowd, "We owe her a major debt of gratitude for her service to our country." The president-elect then turned his attention to America's bright future.

"So it's been what they call a historic event, but to be really historic, we have to do a great job, and I promise you that I will not let you down.... While the campaign is over, our work on this movement is now really just beginning...and we're going to be doing a job that hopefully you will be so proud of your president."

THE REAL ENEMY
In 2016, Trump's chief strategist Steve Bannon said the media, not the Democrats, were "the opposition party."

The Twitter President

Two people are credited with turning Donald Trump on to Twitter: A marketing man named Peter Costanzo, who suggested it to him to promote his book *Think Like a Champion* in 2009; and his ex-wife Ivana. "I said, 'I think you should tweet. It's a new way, a new technology. And if you want to get your words across rightly, without telling *The New York Times*, which is going to twist every single word of yours, this is how you get your message out,'" she told *CBS This Morning*.

A parody account, @DonaldTrump, already existed, so Trump used @realDonaldTrump. He sent his first tweet on May 4, 2009, to promote his appearance on CBS's *Late Show With David Letterman*.

Since then, he's made Twitter his own, amassing 76 million followers and dishing out policy statements, attacks, rebuttals and jokes.

After using it effectively during the campaign, Trump now relies on the platform to directly reach the American people, with his tweets averaging 18,000 retweets and 74,000 likes each. "I'm covered so dishonestly by the press—so dishonestly—that I can put it out on Twitter...I can go bing bing bing...and they put it on [TV] as soon as I tweet it out," Trump's said about his tweeting habit.

"[The media] can't stand the fact that this Administration has done more than virtually any other Administration in its first 2yrs," Trump tweeted in April 2019.

WHITE HOUSE V

ONE'S A 200-YEAR-OLD AMERICAN ICON, THE OTHER'S GILDED IN GOLD: HOW

★ ★ ★ ★ ★

The first lady led a restoration of the Blue Room's furniture.

Thomas Moran's "The Three Tetons" is part of the White House Collection.

AMERICAN STANDARD
The White House receives 6,000 visitors every day—that's 1.25 million a year—and tours are available daily.

Address	1600 Pennsylvania Avenue Washington, D.C.
Year Built	1792
Worth	$90 million
Square Footage	55,000
Number of Floors	4
Style	Neoclassical Federal
Bedrooms/Bathrooms	11/35
The View	Washington Monument
On the Walls	Paintings by American artists from the National Gallery's collection
Amenities	Tennis court, basketball court, pool, bowling lane
Water Feature	Fountains on both the North and South Lawns
Elevators	28

S. TRUMP TOWER

THE FIRST FAMILY'S MANSION IN D.C. COMPARES TO THEIR NYC PENTHOUSE.

725 Fifth Avenue
New York City, New York

1979

$100 million

11,000

3

King Louis XIV's Versailles

7/?

Central Park

Murals of Roman chariots

24-hour concierge, gym

60-foot waterfall wall
in the atrium

1 (34 in the entire building)

NEXT-DOOR NEIGHBORS

The family's penthouse is one of 263 residences inside Trump Tower's 58 stories, a mix of residential and commercial space.

Trump Tower's internal waterfall pours from a pink marble wall.

Trump's penthouse looks out on all of Central Park's 800 acres.

125

TAKING CARE OF BUSINESS
"We've done more than any administration in the first few years," Trump declared in February 2020.

MAKING AMERICA
GREET

★ ★ ★ ★ ★

IN HIS FIRST FOUR YEARS, PRESIDENT DONALD TRUMP HAS MADE GOOD

AGAIN

ON MANY OF HIS CAMPAIGN PROMISES — AND THE COUNTRY IS THRIVING.

WHEN DONALD TRUMP PROMISED
to Make America Great Again, it
wasn't just hot air to get votes. His
plan of action included growing
the economy, reducing taxes for the
middle class, creating 25 million jobs,
ending illegal immigration (and the
swift removal of the millions who
have already entered the country),
just to name a few—and over his
first four years in office, Trump
has impressively made good on his
campaign promise. "From now on,
America will be empowered by our
aspirations," says the president, "not
burdened by our fears; inspired by
the future, not bound by the failures
of the past; and guided by our vision,
not blinded by our doubts."

To his credit, Trump found much
of his success in his very first year.
Throughout 2017, he made the
economy his priority, with the goal
of chipping away at the nation's
$20 trillion deficit by reducing
federal spending and renegotiating
foreign trade deals—and it continues
to be his greatest achievement as
president. When he was elected,
Trump promised to replace NAFTA
(the North American Free Trade
Agreement, between the U.S., Canada

GROWING AMERICA

At a rally in Indiana, Trump showed off Make Our Farmers Great Again hats, which his campaign sells online.

129

IMMIGRATION CRACKDOWN
ICE claims the agency removed more than 267,000 illegal aliens discovered in the U.S. in 2019.

and Mexico) and that October, he met with Canadian Prime Minister Justin Trudeau to discuss new possibilities. The ball got rolling, and by the following year, he proudly announced the revised agreement with a slightly different name, USMCA (United States–Mexico–Canada Agreement), which benefits all three countries involved. Describing it as a "historic transaction," Trump bragged, "I think my biggest concession would be making the deal."

American citizens have also profited from the administration's economic policy, which strives to help them gain wealth and secure their futures by cutting taxes, creating jobs and lowering unemployment. In September 2017, Trump proposed The Tax Cuts Act; signed just two months later on December 22, it provided an astounding $5.5 trillion in cuts, with 60 percent, or $3.2 trillion, going to working families. According to the White

"THE COUNTRY, WHEN I TOOK IT OVER, WAS IN VERY BAD SHAPE."

PRESIDENT TRUMP

45's First 100 Days

TRUMP PLEDGED 28 KEY INITIATIVES IN HIS 100-DAY "CONTRACT WITH THE AMERICAN VOTER." WHAT DID HE ACCOMPLISH BY APRIL 29, 2017?

DAY 1

Repeal Obamacare
Issues Executive Order 13765 to scale back parts of the Affordable Care Act, but a lack of support caused it to stall in Congress.

DAY 5

✓ **Cancel federal funding to sanctuary cities**
Signs Executive Order 13768 to cut funding to sanctuary cities that refuse to comply with his immigration policy.

✓ **Restore public safety and protect law enforcement**
Establishes three key executive orders, one of which put the Attorney General in charge of a task force to reduce crime across America. Four months later, the Restoring Community Safety Act pledged a $175 million increase in law-enforcement spending.

DAY 12

✓ **Select a replacement for Justice Scalia**
Nominates federal appellate judge Neil Gorsuch, a supporter of the right to bear arms (an issue vital to Trump), to the Supreme Court.

DAY 32

✓ **Begin removing illegal immigrants**
Announces the creation of 15,000 jobs in immigration enforcement.

DAY 41

Lift federal restrictions on energy production
Appoints Rick Perry as the U.S. Secretary of Energy—but it's another 119 days until the president called for a review of nuclear energy policy and for increased energy exports.

DAY 68

✓ **Develop comprehensive plan to protect from cyberattacks**
Signs Executive Order 13694, which blocks "the property of certain persons engaging in significant malicious cyber-enabled activities."

DAY 70

✓ **Identify all foreign trading abuses**
Signs two executive orders: one commissioning a study to identify potential cheating and the other to prevent foreign manufacturers from undercutting U.S. companies by selling goods at an unfair price.

DAY 96

✓ **Provide middle-class tax relief**
Releases tax-reform outline plan—with four days to spare before he hit

Trump signed his tax reform act in December 2017.

day 100—although it was another 230 days before the Tax Cuts Act was signed on December 22.

DAY 97

Label China a "currency manipulator"
Changes mind on the matter—but it was only temporary. Trump had accused China of falsifying the value of its yuan since 2011, and he wanted the Department of Treasury make the official declaration. The Bureau eventually did—but not until August 5.

CONFRONTING THE PRESS
CNN's Jim Acosta (pictured) was briefly banned from the White House in November 2018.

THE FIGHT AGAINST FAKE NEWS

If Trump isn't battling Democrats, he's fighting "fake news" about his administration. Ever since his very first press briefing, POTUS has used the catchphrase to combat what he considers the mainstream media's biased misreporting of his presidential activities, with CNN and *The New York Times* being the biggest offenders

Trump first said "fake news" in a December 2016 tweet knocking down a report that he would stay on *The Apprentice*, and he has broadened the term from what he calls inaccurate reporting to anything in the media he disagrees with.

In January 2017, Trump debuted the term at the White House when CNN reporter Jim Acosta asked him to comment about the accusation he was "concocting" a national emergency at the border simply to get 'The Wall' built. "You're CNN, you're fake news," responded Trump. "You have an agenda." When Acosta tried to ask a second question, the president shut him down completely. "Your organization is terrible. I am not going to give you a question. You are fake news." According to Acosta, then-White House press secretary Sean Spicer threatened to throw him out if he made a third attempt.

The incident drew so much press coverage, Trump took to Twitter to decry CNN and the "failing" *New York Times*, as well as NBC, ABC and CBS, for being "the enemy of the American People"—and "fake news" went viral.

Throughout his first term, Trump used "fake" more than 800 times on Twitter alone; at least 650 of the references were specifically to "fake news" (in public, he said "fake" hundreds more times). Besides that phrase, he's also called the mainstream media "scum," "slime," "disgusting" and "dishonest."

House, a family of four earning $75,000 will save more than $2,000 in taxes and their standard deduction nearly doubles. On the job front, unemployment fell from 4.9 percent to 4.4 percent during Trump's first year—and has continued to decrease. By the end of 2019, unemployment had dropped another 30 percent to 3.5 percent, the lowest since 1969.

Trump's first term has welcomed an unprecedented era of economic prosperity, and at the start of 2020, he proudly touted the fruits of his pro-growth agenda: More than seven million jobs have been created, nearly 2.5 million Americans have been lifted out of poverty, job openings have exceeded job seekers for 21 consecutive months, unemployment for women and minorities (blacks, Hispanics and Asians) has reached record lows, and perhaps the most impressive, the bottom half of households have seen their net worth grow by 47 percent—more than three times

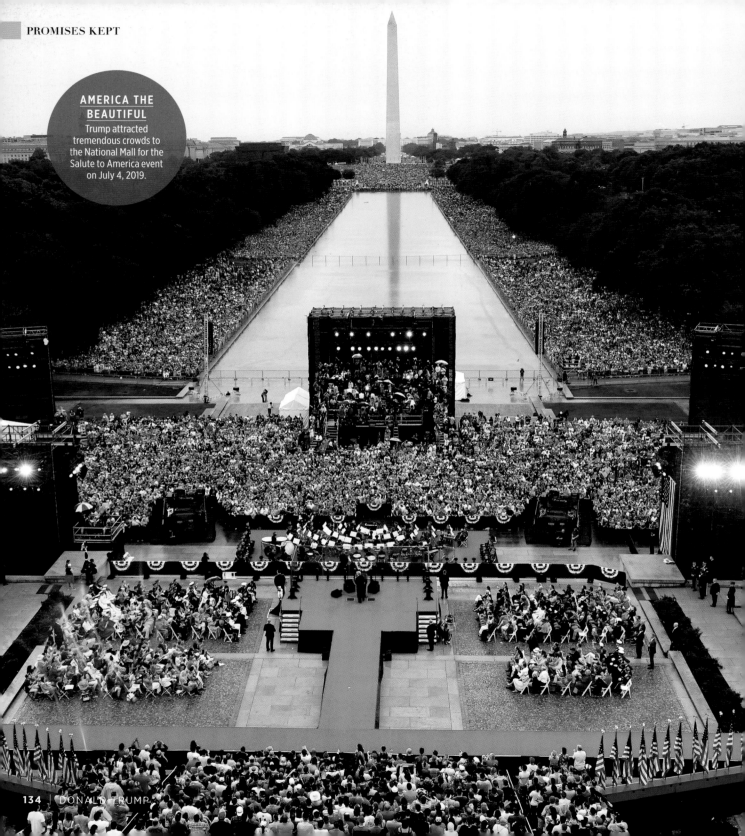

AMERICA THE BEAUTIFUL
Trump attracted tremendous crowds to the National Mall for the Salute to America event on July 4, 2019.

faster than the top 1 percent. "The American Dream is back—bigger, better, and stronger than ever before," boasted Trump. "No one is benefiting more than America's middle class."

A major factor in the president's revitalization of the country is protecting it with an immigration system. A week on the job, he signed Executive Order 13769, which placed restrictions on travel to the U.S. for citizens of seven largely Muslim countries—Iran, Iraq, Libya, Somalia, Sudan, Syria and Yemen—although Iraq was later removed following protests. When Attorney General Sally Yates refused to defend the order in court, Trump fired her and replaced her with someone who would. Since January 2017, he has continued to add more countries to the list, including North Korea, Venezuela and Nigeria.

Illegal immigration has become synonymous with the Trump Administration, as the president has been steadfast in his mission to crack down on the threat against homeland security. The hallmark of his campaign was the wall he promised to build along the U.S.-Mexico border to prevent unauthorized people from immigrating to the U.S. (see sidebar, right). He also devised a plan to remove those who had already slipped through. In September 2017, Trump announced he was canceling Deferred Action for Childhood Arrivals (DACA), Obama's program that allowed an estimated 800,000 young adults who were illegally brought into the country, called

HIGH PRIORITY
Sections of the 30-foot-high wall go up in Yuma, Arizona, the third-busiest area of the U.S.-Mexico border.

Building "The Wall"

Since the very beginning of his presidential campaign, Trump has vowed to crack down on illegal immigration, going as far as to build a physical wall on the U.S.-Mexico border "and make Mexico pay for it." And no sooner was he in office, he got to work on his plan, signing Executive Order 13767, which formally directed the government to begin construction using federal funding (according to an internal report, 'The Wall' was estimated to cost $21.6 billion and take three-and-a-half years to complete). After a number of roadblocks, in July 2019 the Supreme Court finally approved the reallocation of $2.5 billion from the Department of Defense's anti-drug funding, followed by an additional $3.6 billion from military construction projects.

Due to the delay in funding, construction is also behind schedule, but Trump intends to still hit his goal of completing 450 miles by the end of 2020 or by early 2021. "That was a promise," the president's senior adviser and son-in-law Jared Kushner tells Politico, "and it's important that it's now being accomplished."

As of February 2020, 122 miles have been constructed of the wall's reported 1,300-mile length. That same month, Trump noted the portions that had been erected were already proving "100 percent effective." "Illegal border crossings have dropped eight straight months in a row—that's a big number. Illegal crossings are down over 75 percent since last spring."

How Trump Is Fixing "Obama's Mess"

INTERNATIONAL DIPLOMACY
Obama "was begging for a meeting" with Kim Jong-un, but was rejected, Trump claims.

The 45th president wasted no time cleaning up the actions of the 44th. Trump vowed to spend his first day "cancel[ing] every unconstitutional executive action, memorandum and order issued by President Obama." Sure enough, on Day 1, he issued an order to scale back parts of the Affordable Care Act (aka Obamacare), with plans to replace it with his own. (In March 2020, the Supreme Court announced

it would hear the case later in the year, likely after the election.) On Day 5, Trump signed an order to revive the Keystone XL Pipeline, a controversial endeavor to import Canadian oil that Obama had roadblocked his entire presidency. After years of delays, in January 2020, Trump approved a right-of-way allowing the pipeline to be built across U.S. land, pushing the $8 billion project closer to construction.

Outside of America, North Korea's nuclear program has long been a concern for U.S. presidents, but Obama truly let the situation escalate. Months into Obama's first term, North Korea detonated a series of bombs. Instead of negotiating, he imposed "strategic patience" until the communist country was ready to make a good-faith effort with the U.S. They didn't—instead, North Korea launched a series of cyberattacks on American

businesses. And months before the end of Obama's second term, the country again tested a nuclear warhead.

Quite the opposite, in October 2017, Trump used his best weapon against North Korea's leader: Twitter. "Being nice to Rocket Man," his nickname for Kim Jong-un, "hasn't worked in 25 years, why would it work now? Clinton failed, Bush failed, and Obama failed. I won't fail." It was unconventional, but it worked. In June 2018, the two met, an unprecedented move by an American president, resulting in Trump proudly declaring, "There is no longer a nuclear threat from North Korea." A year later, he became the first sitting president to step inside North Korea when he invited Kim to meet at the Korean Demilitarized Zone bordering the nation—and he did. But the truce was short-lived. By the end of 2019, amid stalled denuclearization negotiations, Trump revived "Rocket Man." Despite North Korea continuing its nuclear program, he said, "I have confidence in him. I like him, he likes me, we have a good relationship.... We'll see what happens. It may work out, it may not."

NEW
BEGINNINGS
On June 30, 2019,
Jong-un and Trump
met in Panmunjom, in
the Demilitarized Zone
between the two Koreas.

Trump's no-nonsense approach has also been beneficial in regard to Iran. In 2015, Obama struck a deal to grant the country sanctions relief in return for imposing limits on its nuclear program—but it would expire over the next 12 years. And that was simply unacceptable to Trump. He not only pulled out of the deal in 2018, he introduced the most robust economic sanctions that have ever been placed on Iran. But that wasn't all: In January 2020, he ordered the assassination of its top military commander Qasem Soleimani (see page 172 for more).

Dreamers, to work legally as adults. "I have a love for these people," insisted Trump, "and hopefully now Congress will be able to help them and do it properly." Amid protests from Democrats, Trump didn't back down, but the cancellation was put on hold by a court order, and in 2020, the Supreme Court is expected to make a final ruling.

Trump's immigration policy hit a low note in February 2018 when he imposed "zero tolerance" for anyone caught illegally crossing the border, due to the practice of separating minors from their families, sending children to government shelters and adults to federal jail as they await prosecution. What resulted was a publicity nightmare, as 2,300 children

were depicted living "in cages," fueling a widespread condemnation. Protests popped up in 600 cities across all 50 states, demanding that separated families be reunited. The American Academy of Pediatrics denounced the policy, claiming it would cause "irreparable harm" to migrant children. What the administration hoped would be a deterrent was doing more harm than good—and that June, Trump ordered that unauthorized families caught at the border no longer be separated—and those who had been, to be reunited.

Although the president bore the brunt of the controversy, the federal agency that carried out his order, U.S. Immigration and Customs Enforcement (ICE), also received a fair share, with Democrats calling for its abolishment—but Trump had their back. Praising ICE as "one of the smartest, toughest and most spirited law enforcement groups of men and women that I have ever seen," he assured the agency their jobs were safe in a series of tweets. "You are doing a fantastic job of keeping us safe by eradicating the worst criminal elements. So brave! The radical left Dems want you out. Next it will be all police. Zero chance, It will never happen!" Despite backlash due to the border crisis, according to ICE, fewer unauthorized people have attempted to immigrate to the U.S. In 2019, they reported 143,000 aliens had been arrested, a 10 percent drop from 2018. Also, 86 percent of those arrested had criminal convictions or pending charges for homicide (1,900), sexual offenses (12,000), assault (45,000), drugs (67,000), weapons (10,000) and DUI (74,000).

Trump and ICE were in the crosshairs again in August 2019 when a raid of seven food-processing plants in Mississippi discovered a record 680 undocumented workers. As images and videos of the devastated migrant children were splashed all over the media, critics compared the operation to the 2018 border crisis— but Trump remained resolute on his commitment to immigration. "I want

A PATRIOTIC CELEBRATION

HIS JULY 4, 2019, EVENT THRILLED D.C. CROWDS

Inspired by the Bastille Day events put on for him by French president Emmanuel Macron in 2017, Donald Trump's Independence Day festivities—with the Lincoln Memorial as a backdrop—were every bit as impressive. Highlights included a patriotic speech by Trump, flyovers by every branch of the military, an array of tanks and a dazzling fireworks display.

MILITARY MIGHT
The Navy Blue Angels flyover during the Salute to America event thrilled the crowds in Washington, D.C.

people to know that if they come into the United States illegally, they're getting out," he said. "They're going to be brought out. And this serves as a very good deterrent. When people see what they saw [in Mississippi], like they will be for a long time, they know that they're not staying."

For the 2020 U.S. Census, which collects information about the population to determine federal funds, grants and support to each state, Trump fought to include a question about citizenship that had been removed in 1950. But after the Supreme Court blocked his effort, Trump instead signed an executive order requesting the information come from various government agencies who are able to tap into their existing documents and databases.

"There used to be a time when you could proudly declare, 'I am a citizen of the United States,'" he said. "We will defend the right of the American people to know the full facts about the population size of citizens and non-citizens in America. Unfortunately, this effort was delayed by meritless litigation. As shocking as it may be, far-left Democrats in our country are determined to conceal the number of illegal aliens in our midst. They probably know the number is far greater, much higher than anyone would have believed before. Maybe that's why they fight so hard. This is part of a broader left-wing effort to erode the rights of the American citizen." But, vowed Trump, his administration would not let that happen. "In everything we do, we will faithfully represent the people of the United States of America."

Trump's Latest Real Estate Project: The White House

As redecorating jobs go, it was hardly an extreme makeover, White House edition. After the election, Trump put his stamp on his new digs, getting rid of the modern art favored by Barack and Michelle Obama and replacing it with classic oils of his heroes Teddy Roosevelt and Andrew Jackson. Gone, too, were Obama's burgundy curtains in the Oval Office, swapped out for gold ones last seen during the Clinton Administration.

For a billionaire accustomed to a gold-covered NYC penthouse, that change was modest. Trump kept the Resolute desk, introduced by Jacqueline Kennedy to the Oval Office, and the Bronco Buster cowboy statue that's been around since Lyndon B. Johnson. But Trump says he paid for a huge new chandelier in the dining room out of his own pocket. In fact, of all the rooms in the White House, this was the one that got the most attention, as Trump spends much of his time there reading newspapers and eating meals.

"We found gold behind the walls, which I always knew," Trump told *Time* magazine. "Renovations are grand."

A NEW LOOK
Trump replaced Obama's rug, which had quotes from historical figures, with a rug designed by former first lady Laura Bush.

141

★ ★ ★ ★

AN ORIGINAL
FIRST LADY

THE FOREIGN-BORN MELANIA TRUMP BRINGS HER OWN MODERN BRAND TO THE TRADITIONAL ROLE — AND SHE MAKES NO APOLOGIES ABOUT IT.

LADY OF THE PEOPLE
"She gets no credit from the media," said President Trump, "but she gets credit from the people."

FOREIGN RELATIONS
When Melania visited a school in Nairobi in 2018, she was escorted by Kenya's first lady, Margaret Kenyatta.

DONALD TRUMP ISN'T THE ONLY one who breaks both molds and rules. When his wife, Melania, became first lady of the United States in January 2017, the Slovenian achieved the dual distinction of being the first naturalized citizen in the role, and the first whose native language is not English. Unlike many of her predecessors, she doesn't worry about optics—after all, she's married to one of the most divisive men in the world. And she has her own unique brand:

She can be outspoken, but only when the time is right, always with grace— and she shares her honest thoughts with her powerful husband. "I don't always agree [with] what he tweets, and I tell him that," Melania admitted in 2018. And during the COVID-19 epidemic in early 2020, while her husband said he likely wouldn't wear a protective mask, Melania tweeted a picture of herself in one to promote social distancing. "It's very important for me that I express what I feel," she's

said. "He's the president, but I give him my opinions."

If Melania had any doubts about how she'd fare as first lady, her husband did not. Early in his campaign, Trump boasted he was confident his wife "would be an amazing representative for our country.... I could see her being very involved in women's health issues." Sure enough, the first event Melania hosted at the White House in March 2017 was an invitation-only luncheon

"THOSE HOURS WITH YOUR CHILD ARE REALLY IMPORTANT ONES."

MELANIA TRUMP

Her Passion Project

The welfare of children is near and dear to Melania's heart, and as first lady, she has dedicated her time and energy to a number of causes devoted to the next generation. Her signature campaign, Be Best, focuses on the major issues related to young people through the encouragement of positive social, emotional and physical habits. The three pillars of Be Best are: Well-Being (promoting values such as kindness and respect); Online Safety (cyberbullying); and Opioid Abuse, the latter which has taken on a life of its own as the epidemic cripples the nation.

At a Las Vegas town hall in 2019, Melania encouraged families to educate their children about the dangers of drug use, especially opioids, just as she has with her son, Barron. "I try to explain how drugs are dangerous and it will mess up your head, it will mess up your body and nothing positive comes out of it."

Later that year, Melania brought national attention to another deadly vice sweeping the nation: vaping. Following the president's vow to ban e-cigarettes—which have been linked to tobacco-related disease and death—the first lady called on the U.S. government to take action "and prevent e-cigarettes from becoming an on-ramp to nicotine addiction for a generation of youth."

But Melania believes there's hope to win the war, and she's arming herself with knowledge: She invited a number of teens who have kicked the habit of vaping to the White House, where she listened to their stories and learned firsthand from their experiences—and it's only the beginning, she says: "I'll continue addressing these health concerns to protect our most vulnerable."

celebrating International Women's Day. As her guests dined on tomato-mozzarella salad, thyme-brined chicken, spinach gnocchi and white wine, the first lady shared her story as a female immigrant—and introduced two tenets of her platform: gender equality and women's education.

"Having grown up in a Communist society, I know all too well the value and importance of freedom and equal opportunity—ideals which this great nation was founded

[on] and has continued to strive toward throughout its history," said Melania. "There remains far more brutal and terrifying incarnations of actual gender persecution which we must face together, such as forced enslavement, sexual abuse and absolute repression of far too many women and girls around the globe. We must remember these women in our daily prayers and use our combined resources to help free them from such unthinkable and

inhumane circumstances. I continue to firmly believe that education is the most powerful way to promote and ensure women's rights. Together we will do this not only by striving for gender parity at all levels of education, but also by showing all children, and especially boys, that it is through empathy, respect and kindness that we achieve our collective potential."

The White House is one of three residences the Trumps split their

MOST IMPORTANT JOB: MOTHER

Of all the duties that come with serving as first lady, it's the one at home that's a full-time job. Ever since the Trumps' only child together, Barron, was born in 2006, mother and son have had an unbreakable bond. Even now, as he's grown from a little boy to a strapping 14-year-old, he remains her priority. Before the White House, Melania's goal was to give him as normal a life as possible—and that hasn't changed with him becoming the first son.

Aside from a few appearances at official events and glimpses of him disembarking Air Force One, the Trumps have kept Barron away from the judging glare

of the public to which she and Trump are often subjected. When the president and his family traveled to England in June 2019, for instance, Barron stayed home. "This is not normal life," Melania told Fox News' Sean Hannity in 2018. "But I like to protect him and give him the childhood he deserves." Unlike most young people, the teen is not on social media, either.

Melania is so protective of Barron, she uncharacteristically spoke out about him when a Stanford Law professor testifying at President Trump's impeachment trial made a joke about her son's name ("While the president

Barron attended the 2017 Easter Egg Roll at the White House.

can name his son Barron, he can't make him a baron"). "A minor child deserves privacy and should be kept out of politics," the first lady sounded off in a fiery tweet

to her 13 million followers. "Pamela Karlan, you should be ashamed of your very angry and obviously biased public pandering, and using a child to do it."

ROYAL TREATMENT
At Buckingham Palace, Melania chatted with Queen Elizabeth II at a reception for NATO leaders in 2019.

A SYMBOL OF FRIENDSHIP
In 2018, Trump and French President Emmanuel Macron planted a French oak tree on the White House Lawn.

In October 2019, Melania visited Wyoming, where she rafted on the Snake River with schoolchildren.

> ## "YOU JUDGE A SOCIETY BY HOW IT TREATS ITS CITIZENS."
>
> MELANIA TRUMP

time among (including Trump Tower in New York City and Mar-a-Lago in South Florida), but Melania has taken an active role at 1600 Pennsylvania Avenue, planning state dinners and keeping tabs on her husband's diet.

According to CNN reporter Kate Bennett, who spent three years embedded in the first lady's East Wing for her 2019 unauthorized biography *Free, Melania*, an average day includes creating guest lists for luncheons and going over décor (at her International Women's Day soiree, visitors were especially wowed with the floral arrangements of tulips and sweet peas that adorned the State Dining Room). "It is, essentially, a wealthy woman's life, and that is basically what she was: a wealthy, stay-at-home mom with

three homes," Bennett said in an interview with *The Cut*. "And thinking about, 'Oh God, it's already August, we have to start thinking about the Thanksgiving table arrangements.' For her that's a very real workday."

The first lady has also been dedicated to the issues that are most important to her, especially those involving America's youngest citizens (see "Her Passion Project," page 145). Every Valentine's Day for three years running, Melania has celebrated the holiday of love with patients at The Children's Inn at NIH (National Institutes of Health) in Bethesda, Maryland. During her 2020 visit, the red-leather-clad Melania handed out valentines and hugs, decorated heart-shaped cookies and answered important questions like, "How many

SOLO TRIP
In October 2018, during a weeklong visit to Africa, Melania met these children from the Nest orphanage in Nairobi, Kenya.

rooms are in the White House?" The children also showered her with gifts, including a bouquet of roses and a handmade picture frame, which she promised she'd put in her office at the White House. "Spending time at [the Children's Inn] with the inspiring & beautiful children on #ValentinesDay has become a treasured tradition of mine," she tweeted later that day. "It was a wonderful day to share love & kindness with these strong warriors!"

It's not only the welfare of American children that concerns Melania. In October 2018, she took her Be Best campaign international for a weeklong mission in Africa. Without her husband by her side, Melania's little-seen personality shined: In Nairobi, as she bottle-fed orphaned elephants at a sanctuary, the usually restrained first lady laughed loudly as she petted the animals and tickled their ears. At a school in Malawi, the third-poorest country in the world, she shared a book with a little boy during his lesson, and then presented the teachers with Be Best tote bags brimming with much-needed school supplies. In Nairobi, as children at The Nest orphanage serenaded her, Melania danced along—the first time anyone had seen her move like that since her husband's Inauguration.

That solo trip was a rare peek at the real Melania Trump, says Kate Andersen Brower, author of *First Women: The Grace and Power of America's Modern First Ladies*. "Reporters who covered Hillary Clinton when she was first lady told me she became more open and likable the farther she was from Washington, and I think the same is true of this first lady. But she is so much more guarded than Hillary Clinton—which is hard to believe—and so I think, for [Melania], this was as transparent and open as we may ever see her."

Despite comparisons to Clinton, Trump really models herself after Jacqueline Kennedy. Before her husband was even elected, Melania admitted she would be "traditional," like the wife of John F. Kennedy. There's no denying she's as glamorous as her—and the president agrees. "We have our own Jackie O. today," he bragged. "We'll call it Melania T."

The 45th first lady is in a class all her own. Melania—whose Secret Service code name is "Muse" (Trump's is "Mogul," naturally)—employs a rather small staff of 10, less than half of previous first ladies. Her inner circle is even tighter: "She has, like, three people around her," reveals Bennett. But that's exactly how Melania likes it. "I have the same group of friends I had before," she told *ABC News* in 2018. "And I always prefer quality over quantity."

The traits that make Melania not the average first lady are the things that define her as an originator in the role. "The secret to Melania Trump's confidence and to her survival as first lady?" asks Bennett in the introduction of her biography. "She doesn't care what anyone thinks about her. Whether people assume she is complicit in Trump's beliefs and actions by being married to him…or whether they think she is standing by his side because she is a noble adherent to traditional marriage—it doesn't matter to her."

Her Best White House Looks

Melania Trump's natural fashion flair, a leftover from her days as a model, has served her well in the White House. She tends to wear classic, elegant pieces, but always with an interesting twist—an eye-catching color, a pretty print or a fashion-forward silhouette. She favors designers including Dior, Givenchy, Carolina Herrera, Gucci, Fendi and Dolce & Gabbana. Like most first ladies, Melania pays for her clothes out-of-pocket; under ethics rules, first ladies *can* receive free designer clothes, but the togs then become government property and are sent to the National Archives.

FASHION FIRESTORM
Outrage erupted on social media when Melania wore a $39 Zara jacket that read "I Really Don't Care. Do U?" while visiting a Texas immigration detention facility in 2018. After first denying there was any hidden message, Melania later revealed to ABC News that the words were meant "for the people and for the left-wing media who are criticizing me. And I want to show them that I don't care." Point to Melania!

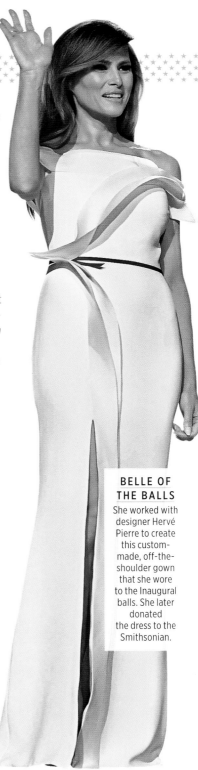

BELLE OF THE BALLS
She worked with designer Hervé Pierre to create this custom-made, off-the-shoulder gown that she wore to the Inaugural balls. She later donated the dress to the Smithsonian.

FALL FASHIONISTA

The first lady was on trend in brown suede, matching a Burberry trench with knee-high boots at the 2019 Thanksgiving turkey pardoning.

PRETTY IN PINK

Melania welcomed the Colombian president and first lady to the White House in this $3,570 hot-pink Fendi coat.

MY FAIR LADY

To meet the Queen of England in 2019, Melania looked classic in a white Dolce & Gabbana dress with navy accents and a Hervé Pierre hat.

ORANGE IS THE NEW HOT

Melania stood out at the 2019 G20 summit in Japan in this $1,243 Dries Van Noten print coat.

A ROYAL AFFAIR

For a dinner with Prince Charles and the Duchess of Cornwall during the state visit to the U.K., Melania wore a scene-stealing $8,340 red Givenchy cape dress.

GRAPHIC STATEMENT

This $9,000 Dior coat with an art deco–inspired pattern added some high style to the 2018 turkey pardoning.

THE PEOPLE'S
PRESIDENT

★ ★ ★ ★ ★

FROM KANYE WEST AND KID ROCK TO HIS FERVENT FANS ALL ACROSS THE NATION, DONALD TRUMP HAS RESONATED WITH A WIDE ARRAY OF FOLKS.

KANYE WEST

The rapper's clique usually includes the likes of Jay-Z, Beyoncé, Rihanna and Justin Bieber, but in 2018 he extended it to President Trump. "We are both dragon energy," West tweeted that April. "He is my brother." Six months later, the two put on quite a show in the Oval Office when West—wearing a Make America Great Again hat because "it made me feel like Superman"— went on a 10-minute monologue about hydrogen planes, alternative universes, Adidas and entertainment as an American export in front of the stunned president, his daughter Ivanka and a throng of press gathered to chronicle the spectacle. "If he don't look good, we don't look good," West said, pounding his fist on Trump's desk for effect. "This our president!"

When he came up for air, Trump was speechless. "I'll tell you what," he told reporters. "That was pretty impressive." The two friends even sealed their bond with an embrace. "I love this guy right here," gushed the rapper. "Let me give this guy a hug."

155

KID ROCK

One of President Trump's earliest supporters, the Republican rocker praised his "entertaining" 2016 campaign and noted a businessman was exactly what the government needed.

And once Trump was elected, the two grew even closer, with Kid Rock speaking at the White House in October 2018 when he was on hand to witness the president sign the Music Modernization Act, which amends copyright law and aids music creators in receiving proper royalties.

Over the years since, Kid Rock has become golf buddies with the "so down-to-earth" POTUS, as well as his son Don Jr. In January 2020, the two hit the links at Trump International in Palm Beach, Florida, with the musician dressed down in a T-shirt that mocked Rep. Adam Schiff, one of the Democrats at the center of the impeachment scandal. "Love the shirt buddy," Don Jr. captioned a photo of the two on Instagram. "We are waiving the golf course dress code/policy for that one."

DENNIS RODMAN

It wasn't the best of beginnings between the NBA bad boy and Trump: Rodman's drinking and erratic behavior got him fired from *The Celebrity Apprentice* in 2009. Four years later, he was brought

AMERICAN BADA$$
"Uh oh, I got the mic," joked Kid Rock during a visit to the White House, before going on to praise the president.

LEFT Ted Nugent (at a Trump rally) describes the president as "a hell-raisin', We the People, Constitution, Bill of Rights, be the best that you can be" type of leader.

"LET'S RUN AMERICA LIKE A BUSINESS, WHERE NO COLORS MATTER. WHOEVER CAN DO THE JOB, GETS THE JOB." MIKE TYSON

HEAVY HITTER
Retired baseball star Johnny Damon joined the Trump administration's Sports Council, with the goal to increase youth participation.

back for the all-star edition, but The Donald terminated him for misspelling Melania's name on an ad campaign. After Rodman endorsed Trump for president, though, the two mended fences—and tried to bring about world peace in the process.

Kim Jong-un is good friends with the basketball star, who played an important role, albeit an unofficial one, when he helped facilitate the historic meeting between the North Korean leader and the U.S. president. Rodman was so overjoyed with the result, he sobbed throughout interviews with both ABC News and CNN (while wearing a MAGA hat). Ahead of Trump and Jong-un's

second summit, Rodman praised the president in a public letter: "You are on the cusp of a big, beautiful deal. One that would make you the front-runner for a Nobel Peace Prize without question. You have my forever and forever support!"

TED NUGENT
Like Kid Rock, the "Cat Scratch Fever" singer has been a longtime supporter, and after Trump was elected, the two enjoyed a VIP tour of the White House (and mocked a portrait of Hillary Clinton along with Sarah Palin). What does Nugent think about the job his pal has done? "The best president I have ever seen.

I think Donald Trump's doing a great job. He represents the heart and soul of the heart and soul of this country—the heartland of this country: the farmers, the ranchers, the private property owners, the entrepreneurs, working-hard, playing-hard Americans who earn their own way, live within their means, save for a rainy day, take risks and make sacrifices to be in the asset column."

JOHNNY DAMON
Another *Celebrity Apprentice* contestant who backed his former boss' run for the presidency was former New York Yankees center

More Celebrity Supporters

Loretta Lynn

"What he says he's going to do, I think he can do," the country star told *Time* magazine. She later slammed Madonna and Ashley Judd for taking part in the Women's Marches in protest against Trump, saying, "For God's sake, march if you want to, but do it with class."

Kelsey Grammer

The actor has expressed support of Trump's policies and an admiration for his never-say-die stances. "We've witnessed in American politics the same basic language since Ronald Reagan has been attached to every conservative president, but [Donald Trump] is the first guy that ever fires back...," he said.

Stephen Baldwin

Like Saul of Tarsus (aka Saint Paul), Trump is "God's chosen instrument, whether we like it or not," said the actor and Christian evangelist, whose brother Alec impersonates Trump on *Saturday Night Live*.

Antonio Sabato Jr.

"Donald Trump believes in one America with liberty and justice for all," the actor said at the Republican National Convention in 2016. "Donald Trump will get it done and put us back on the right track."

Trace Adkins

The country singer, who also appeared on *Celebrity Apprentice*, endorsed Trump and caught up with the president in June 2018. "It was like we'd just seen each other last week. He came in and saw my daughter and gave her a hug, and you know, he was just loud and sucked all the air out of the room like he always does," the "Honky Tonk Badonkadonk" singer told WDEZ with a laugh. "Nothing different, same guy as on *The Apprentice*."

fielder Johnny Damon. During a rally in Orlando, Florida, during the 2016 campaign, Damon was in attendance, cheering and waving a MAGA sign—and he even addressed the crowd to explain why they should vote for Trump: "He likes to win, he likes everything to be great, not just for him but for everybody, and he wants to make America great again." And that's exactly what the MLB champion thinks Trump has achieved as president. "I think he's doing a great job," Damon said in 2018. "Sometimes he says things that people don't agree with, but he's not there to be your friend, he's there to run our country."

Sarah Palin shared this photo of her 2017 White House visit with Kid Rock and Ted Nugent on social media.

AN HONOR AND A PRIVILEGE

Mike Pence describes Donald Trump's vice presidential nomination as the "greatest honor of my life."

RIGHT-HAND MAN

AS PRESIDENT TRUMP CONCENTRATES ON MAKING AMERICA GREAT AGAIN, VICE PRESIDENT MIKE PENCE HAS ALWAYS BEEN THERE TO HELP.

THE PRESIDENT CAN ONLY DO SO much. Fortunately for Trump, he has a true teammate in Vice President Mike Pence. During the 2016 campaign, the conservative Indiana governor was the convincing factor for voters in traditional states who might not have been onboard with an unconventional candidate like Trump. And in the White House, he jumped into shaping the administration's foreign policy.

Before Trump chose Pence as his running mate, his other two options were former House Speaker Newt Gingrich and New Jersey Gov. Chris Christie—but Pence aligned with the GOP hopeful on a number of key topics, especially immigration. Following Trump's controversial remarks about a Muslim ban and the wall, Pence went on Fox News in July 2016 to publicly back the Republican nominee: "I want folks to know I strongly agree with Donald Trump; we have to do something different."

During the campaign, Pence—considered the most conservative VP in the past four decades—revealed that Dick Cheney, who served under George W. Bush, was his role model, and like him, he hoped to also be "a

WONDER WOMEN
Karen Pence and Melania Trump greet military schoolchildren at Fort Bragg in North Carolina.

Melania's Second Lady

KAREN PENCE WORKS WITH THE FIRST LADY, AND HAS ALSO STUMPED FOR TRUMP.

Like the president, the first lady has a support system in the Pence family: the VP's wife of 35 years, Karen.

The two women share a passion for young people and have joined forces a number of times to bring awareness to issues near and dear to their hearts, like the military and their families. Over the years, Melania and Karen have assembled care packages for troops overseas and visited children at bases across the U.S.

The second lady has also lent her time to Trump's 2020 campaign, with Mrs. Pence focused on "Women for Trump" events, even headlining her own fundraiser in Iowa. "Mike likes to say, 'If you want hundreds, you invite Mike Pence. If you want thousands, you invite Donald Trump.' So for me, it's maybe like 100 or 200." Still, she'll spread the message to whoever will listen. "I think there are people out there who feel like they know me, so when they hear me say something, maybe it reassures them," says Karen. "Because I see a president who cares about his country."

The first and second ladies toured South Carolina's Joint Base Charleston in October 2019.

very active vice president." And once he was sworn in on January 20, 2017, he got right to work. After ceremonial duties like administering the oath of office to the White House senior staff, Pence had his first introduction to his position as international mediator, sitting in on the president's calls with foreign leaders Russian President Vladimir Putin and Australian Prime Minister Malcolm Turnbull. "The job of the vice president," notes Pence, "is to stand right next to the president and implement the policy that he's decided, and I'm prepared to do that."

Three months later, he set off on his first global tour on behalf of Trump—and laid the groundwork for a historical moment for the president. Pence's 10-day trip throughout Asia began in South Korea, where he met with President Hwang Kyo-ahn to

"HE IS THE RIGHT MAN FOR THE JOB."

PRESIDENT TRUMP, ON PENCE

reaffirm the country's alliance with the U.S. Just hours earlier, North Korea had launched a failed missile test, shifting the VP's focus to the neighboring nation. Pence pledged 100 percent "unwavering support" to South Korea, while warning its northern rival that the "era of strategic patience is over" with Trump in the White House. "North Korea would do well not to test his resolve— or the strength of the armed forces of the United States in this region." Pence continued that message into

Tokyo, where he promised Japanese Deputy Prime Minister Taro Aso that the Trump Administration was working with its Asian allies (Japan, South Korea and China) to dismantle North Korea's nuclear weapons and ballistic missile programs, which he described as "the most dangerous and urgent threat to the peace and security of the Asia Pacific."

Over the following months, Pence continued to work hard toward his goal. The VP, along with his wife, Karen, served as the presidential delegation to the 2018 Olympic Winter Games in Pyeongchang and represented the U.S. at the opening ceremony. While there, Pence also participated in bilateral meetings with leaders from Seoul, South Korea, and Tokyo to discuss security and stability on the Korean Peninsula. In May 2018, North Korea released three American citizens who had been held prisoner for more than a year, an achievement that Pence called "one of the greatest joys of my life" in an interview with ABC News. "I think it is a direct result of President Trump's leadership on the world stage…and we hope it opens the way to a lasting peace." Sure enough, weeks later, Trump and Kim

HOME BASE
Since 1974, this house, on the grounds of the United States Naval Observatory in D.C., has been the official home of the vice president.

SUPPORTING THE TROOPS
VP Pence poses for a selfie with American soldiers onboard the *USS Ronald Reagan* in Yokosuka, Japan.

Trump puts a comforting hand on Pence's thigh during a memorial service for Reverend Billy Graham in February 2018.

Jong-un came together in a historical summit in Singapore, resulting in the North Korean leader's commitment to work toward denuclearization.

The duo of Trump and Pence has adhered to a "good cop, bad cop" approach—with the president and vice president playing interchangeable roles when necessary. If Trump's tough talk ruffles the feathers of allies, Pence swoops in as "the sort of Vaseline after the burn wound," explains former U.S. ambassador to Panama John Feeley. Other times, it's the VP's job to be the "skunk at the garden party," like he did with Mexico's foreign affairs secretary Marcelo Ebrard, who appealed to Pence after Trump threatened tariffs on imports if the country didn't block the flow of migrants illegally entering the U.S. Still, some foreign leaders actually prefer to meet with diplomatic Pence versus Trump.

On the home front, Pence also acts as a bridge between the president and congressional Republicans. Before he was governor, he spent 12 years as a member of the U.S. House of Representatives—and he has brought that expertise to the administration of a man with no prior political experience. Pence had a heavy hand in shaping Trump's cabinet with the appointments of Seema Verma (administrator of the Centers for Medicare and Medicaid Services), Kansas Rep. Mike Pompeo (secretary of state), South Carolina Gov. Nikki Haley (U.S. ambassador to the United Nations) and Georgia

Rep. Tom Price (secretary of Health and Human Services).

Even in times of trouble, Pence has never wavered in his support of the president. When Ukraine's investigation into Joe Biden and his son Hunter turned into an overnight scandal, the VP doubled down on the allegations against his predecessor (see more on page 166). "I think [that] is worth looking into," said Pence. "When you hold the second-highest office in the land it comes with unique responsibilities—not just to be above impropriety, but to be above the appearance of impropriety, and clearly in this case there are legitimate questions that ought to be asked." During the subsequent impeachment trial, the House Intelligence Committee issued a subpoena to Pence, but he refused to turn over any related documents.

As Trump prepares for the 2020 election, his loyal VP has picked up any slack out on the campaign trail. Pence spent the beginning of the year on a national bus tour, drumming up support at several Keep America Great rallies. "You heard it from me," he told a crowd in Troy, Michigan. "President Donald Trump is the real deal. He's never stopped fighting for the people of Michigan and now it's our turn to fight for him. With your continued support, every day between now and November 4, we're going to keep on winning."

MADE IN THE U.S.A.
"Manufacturing is back," Pence declared at a visit to Merit Medical in Utah to promote Trump's USMCA trade deal.

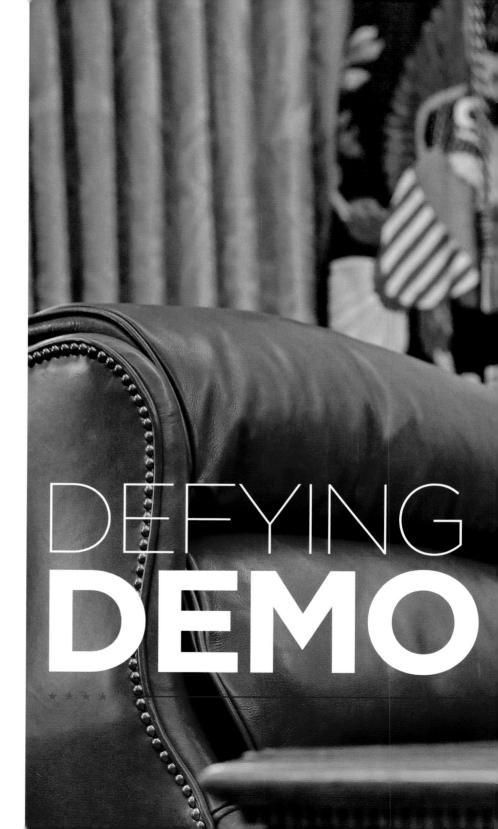

AS HE PREPARED FOR THE 2020 election, President Trump took a closer look at his Democratic competition, namely Joe Biden. The biggest red flag with the former vice president was a questionable (and very high-paying) role granted to his son Hunter at Ukrainian gas company Burisma Holdings in 2014—coincidentally, during the Obama administration's diplomatic overtures to the country. And five years later, Trump wanted answers.

In a July 2019 phone call to President Volodymyr Zelenskyy, Trump brought up suspicions surrounding the Bidens, in particular the VP's efforts in the 2015 firing of Ukraine's top prosecutor Viktor Shokin, who had led an investigation into Burisma. "There's a lot of talk about Biden's son," said Trump, "that Biden stopped the prosecution and a lot of people want to find out about that." His suggestion to Zelenskyy: Ukraine should look into possible corruption, as well as Hunter's $50,000-a-month consultant position at Burisma (his five-year contract ended in April 2019).

To assist in the investigation, Trump offered the services of U.S. Attorney General William Barr and

DEFYING DEMO

CRATS

EVEN AS HE FACED IMPEACHMENT, PRESIDENT TRUMP REFUSED TO BACK DOWN FROM THE LIBERAL "WITCH HUNT GARBAGE" — AND IN THE END, HE WAS ACQUITTED ON ALL CHARGES.

his personal lawyer, former New York City Mayor Rudy Giuliani. Zelenskyy agreed, saying he would look into the Bidens and "restore the honesty" to the situation. But two days before the Ukrainian president planned to announce the investigation on CNN, news broke about a whistleblower's complaint regarding Trump's call—and Democrats jumped at the chance to use it against their rival.

Immediately, liberal leaders rushed toward impeachment, with House Speaker Nancy Pelosi spending her weekend burning up the phone lines with other Democrats to gauge their

Capitalizing on Impeachment

Long before President Trump was acquitted, he was already beating the Democrats.

The impeachment process, labeled as a "transparent effort to interfere with the 2020 election," according to Trump's campaign manager Brad Parscale, actually played right into the president's reelection strategy: Within minutes of Nancy Pelosi's inquiry announcement, Republicans began fundraising off it—and in the last quarter of 2019 alone, Trump's campaign raked in $46 million. "Democrats and the media have been in a sham impeachment frenzy," noted Parscale. "The misguided Democratic impeachment strategy is meant to appease their rabid, extreme, leftist base, but will only serve to embolden and energize President Trump's supporters and create a landslide victory."

opinion. That Monday, as Trump also came under fire for withholding $391 million in military aide from Ukraine during its investigation, he defended his decision: "We're supporting a country. We want to make sure that country is honest. It's very important to talk about corruption. If you don't talk about corruption, why would you give money to a country that you think is corrupt?" Trump also denied blocking the whistleblower's complaint and told Pelosi the White House would release the document,

deposing witnesses in both private and public hearings and without cooperation from the White House. During the investigation, Trump took every opportunity to call out their missteps. In a December 17 letter to Pelosi, he blasted her party's actions. "I have been denied the most fundamental rights afforded by the Constitution, including the right to present evidence, to have my own counsel present, to confront accusers, and to call and cross-examine witnesses. More due process was

on the jury (see more at right). And when their votes were cast, it wasn't even close: The first article failed 48-52 with the second falling even shorter, with 47-53. "It is, therefore, ordered and adjudged," stated Supreme Chief Justice John Roberts, "that the said Donald John Trump be, and he is hereby, acquitted of the charges."

The Democrats' attempt to take down Trump was a colossal failure, and he could hardly wait to celebrate. Within minutes of the verdict, he tweeted he'd make a statement the next day at the White House on "the Impeachment Hoax." But before the public display, he put on a private one that morning at the annual National Prayer Breakfast—with Pelosi on the same stage, no less. "As everybody knows, my family, our great country and your president have been put through a terrible ordeal by some very dishonest and corrupt people," he told the assembly of politicians and religious figures. Next, at the event in the East Room, the mood was lighter, as the president drew laughs when he held up a newspaper with "Trump Acquitted" splashed across its front page. "It's the only good headline I've ever had in *The Washington Post*," he joked.

On a serious note, he warned, it may not be the last time the "vicious as hell" Democrats attempt to remove him. "If they find that I happened to walk across the street and maybe go against the light or something, 'Let's impeach him.' So we'll probably have to do it again because these people have gone stone-cold crazy."

"IT WAS A WHOLE FAKE DEAL AND EVERYBODY KNOWS THAT."
PRESIDENT TRUMP, ON IMPEACHMENT

as well as a transcript of his call with Zelenskyy, by the end of the week.

But she didn't give him the chance: Within hours, on September 24, 2019, Pelosi announced the impeachment inquiry against the president—even though polls revealed half of the country didn't support it. "It simply confirms that House Democrats' priority is not making life better for the American people," scolded Senate Majority Leader Mitch McConnell.

Despite a shaky case, the Democrat-controlled House pushed ahead with their "total witch hunt,"

afforded to those accused in the Salem Witch Trials." The next day, the House voted in favor of impeachment on two articles— abuse of power and obstruction of Congress—although all Republican (and five Democratic) representatives voted against the charges.

On January 16, 2020, Trump's trial commenced in the Republican-controlled Senate, who would decide if he be removed from office or not—and justice was swift. In just 20 days, the prosecution and defense presented their cases to the 53 Republicans and 47 Democrats

Trump has said Adam Schiff (center) made up the whistleblower's complaint.

IMPEACHMENT TRIAL: MEET THE COURT

JUDGE

Supreme Court Chief Justice John Roberts (who was nominated by President George W. Bush in 2005), presided over the impeachment trial, maintaining order, recognizing members to speak and keeping proceedings on schedule. On January 29, senators engaged in a question-and-answer session, with Roberts reading approved inquiries aloud for the court—but there was one in particular from Rand Paul he would not allow: What is the whistleblower's name? (Paul later revealed that identity during a speech.) In his final act as judge on February 5, Roberts announced the verdict on each article of impeachment.

JURY

Although all 100 senators made up the jury, they were guided by leaders from both parties: the majority Republican (Mitch McConnell) and minority Democratic (Chuck Schumer). Going into the trial, the two were already at odds: McConnell called for a swift process with no witnesses, while Schumer wanted a full trial that included testimonies. On the Senate floor, McConnell presented trial procedures, which would end with a vote whether to consider new information (i.e., witness testimony) before the final vote on articles. Schumer deemed the plan a "national disgrace" that rushed the trial without evidence.

PROSECUTION

Seven House managers comprised the prosecution team who tried Trump, led by House Intelligence Committee chairman Adam Schiff and including (above, from left) Hakeem Jeffries, Jerrold Nadler, Val Demings, Sylvia Garcia, Zoe Lofgren and Jason Crow—all members of Congress chosen for their legal and national security experience. For three days, they took turns presenting the prosecution's case for all articles using evidence from the House impeachment inquiry, until January 24, when Schiff rested their case. In his closing remarks, Schiff pleaded with senators to allow for witnesses and documents: "I implore you —give America a fair trial."

DEFENSE

In his impeachment trial, Trump was defended by a dream team of high-profile lawyers, including White House Counsel, his own private counsel, former Florida Attorney General Pam Bondi, and Ken Starr, best known for investigating the Clinton administration's Whitewater controversy—in addition to eight House Republicans. Led by the White House's Pat Cipollone and Jay Sekulow, the defense went after the Bidens, citing their presumed corruption as the reason for the president's actions. The legal team also argued Democrats lacked direct evidence of wrongdoing and were using the impeachment as leverage to beat Trump in the election.

★ ★ ★ ★ ★

WAR ON TERRORISM

PRESIDENT TRUMP PROMISED TO MAKE AMERICA SAFE AGAIN — AND IN HIS FIRST TERM HE ACHIEVED THAT GOAL WITH THE ASSASSINATION OF TWO HIGH-PROFILE TERRORISTS.

BIG VICTORY
From the Situation Room, Trump watched the death of ISIS' Baghdadi, whom he described as "whimpering and crying."

EVER SINCE THE REAGAN

Administration, the U.S. has been embroiled in a war on terror in the Middle East, when Islamic Jihad took responsibility for the 1983 bombing of a Marine Corps barracks in Beirut that killed 241. Over the four decades since, each president has fought their own battle: George H. W. Bush hunted Iraq president Saddam Hussein in the Gulf War; Bill Clinton nearly captured al-Qaeda leader Osama bin Laden; George W. Bush retaliated against the September 11 attack by invading Iraq on a mission for weapons of mass destruction resulting in the arrest of Hussein (who was executed in 2006); Barack Obama ordered the 2011 raid that exterminated bin Laden.

And when Donald Trump took office, he vowed to win the war once and for all. In his inauguration speech, he proclaimed his national security plan to "unite the civilized world against Radical Islamic Terrorism, which we will eradicate completely from the face of the Earth."

Within days, he made his first move. Following Iran's missile test, Trump punished "the rogue regime" by imposing 25 trade sanctions and lobbying European officials to do the same. As tensions intensified, the president withdrew from the Joint Comprehensive Plan of Action (JCPOA), a negotiation between the U.S., U.K., China, France, Germany and Russia to lift sanctions crucial to Iran's economy in exchange for restrictions on its nuclear program.

Now, Trump pledged, the U.S. would wind down business with Iran, culminating in total termination

"He died like a coward," Trump said of ISIS leader Abu Bakr al-Baghdadi, 48.

The attack on Iran's Qasem Soleimani, 62, was so violent, it tore apart his body.

by the end of 2018. When allies attempted to change his mind, he was resolute that Iran face consequences. "If we do nothing, we know exactly what will happen.... The world's leading state sponsor of terror will be on the cusp of acquiring the world's most dangerous weapons."

His prediction was all too real. As Iran's economy took a major hit, President Hassan Rouhani issued an ultimatum: If the world powers didn't devise a new deal to aid Iran within 60 days, the country would begin keeping larger amounts of enriched uranium, instead of exporting the excess per JCPOA—a thinly veiled threat that it would use the chemical to develop a nuclear weapon. Trump maintained his stance, and less than two weeks later,

Iran seemingly retaliated when a rocket landed less than a mile from the U.S Embassy in Baghdad. "If Iran wants to fight," Trump tweeted, "that will be the official end of Iran."

But instead of backing down, Iran escalated matters. The following month, a U.S. military drone was shot down by Islamic Revolutionary Guard Corps, who claimed it was in Iranian airspace—a "clear message," said commander Hossein Salami, that Iran is "completely ready" for war. By the end of 2019, danger truly seemed imminent: On December 31, members and supporters of pro-Iranian paramilitary groups smashed the front door of the U.S. Embassy in Baghdad and staged a sit-in that lasted for days. Trump had seen enough. "Iran will be held fully responsible for lives lost, or damage incurred, at any of our facilities," he tweeted. "They will pay a very BIG PRICE! This is not a Warning."

Forty-eight hours later, in a predawn airstrike, top military commander Qasem Soleimani was assassinated by an American drone in Baghdad. He may not be one of the more familiar names associated with terrorism, but Soleimani's reach was wide: He oversaw Iran's operation in the Syrian Civil War, working closely with President Bashar al-Assad in the massacre of his people. According to Trump, Soleimani was plotting to do more harm at U.S. embassies. "We caught a total monster."

As mourners demanded revenge, Trump warned of retaliation against Americans or U.S. assets: 52 Iranian sites would be targeted, one for every American held hostage during the

1979 seizure of the U.S. Embassy in Tehran. President Rouhani made a greater threat. "Those who refer to the number 52 should also remember the number 290," the number of Iranians killed when the U.S. accidentally shot down a passenger plane in 1988 (see "America's History With Iran" on page 177 for more).

Following Soleimani's funeral, Rouhani did follow through with assaults on two U.S. air bases in Iran, but they were remarkably inconsequential—four missiles missed targets completely—with no casualties and only minimal damage. As tensions de-escalated, Trump remained vigilant. "As long as I am president of the United States, Iran will never be allowed to have a nuclear weapon."

But Iran was not the only terrorist hotbed. Months into Trump's presidency, amid the Syrian civil war, a massive nerve gas attack killed 89 people and injured another 500. That night, Trump condemned "dictator" President Assad for the massacre and called on "all civilized nations to join us in seeking to end this slaughter and bloodshed in Syria and also to end terrorism of all kinds and all types." For its part, the U.S. launched a defensive attack: Navy destroyers fired dozens of cruise missiles at the Syrian Air Force base suspected of the chemical warfare, targeting aircraft, storage areas and ammunition supply bunkers. The operation was lauded by Republicans and Democrats alike, including two of his biggest critics at the time, senators John McCain and Lindsey Graham. "Unlike the previous administration, President Trump confronted a pivotal moment in Syria and took action," they said in a joint

UNITED BY TERRORISM
In 2018, President Trump presided over a United Nations Security Council meeting in New York City.

"THE U.S. IS READY TO EMBRACE PEACE WITH ALL WHO SEEK IT." PRESIDENT TRUMP

NEVER FORGET
On the 18th anniversary of the 9/11 terrorist attack that killed nearly 3,000 Americans, the Trumps observed a moment of silence.

statement. "For that, he deserves the support of the American people."

McCain and Graham also urged Trump to "take Assad's air force... completely out of the fight." One year later, he did just that in a combined operation with Britain and France, following a second deadly gassing against civilians. "These are not the actions of a man," said Trump. "They are crimes of a monster." And in April 2018, the president and his allies handed out Assad's punishment: a precision military strike twice the size of the last, which took out the heart of his chemical weapons. Eight months later, Trump officially declared victory. "We have defeated ISIS in Syria," he tweeted on December 19, 2018, "my only reason for being there during the Trump Presidency."

There were still some lingering ISIS strongholds, though, particularly Abu Bakr al-Baghdadi, a depraved murderer, serial rapist and the world's No. 1 terrorist leader. Capturing or killing Baghdadi was the top national security priority for the Trump Administration, and after several years on the run, he was tracked down in northwest Syria. In a daring October 2019 raid, U.S. Special Operations forces hunted down Baghdadi, who retreated to a tunnel. When he reached a dead end, he detonated a suicide vest, killing himself and three of his children who he had dragged with him. "A brutal killer, one who has caused so much hardship and death, was violently eliminated—he will never again harm another innocent man, woman or child," said Trump. "The world is now a much safer place."

America's History With Iran

1953
Two years after the election of Prime Minister Mohammad Mosaddegh, the CIA assists Britain in a coup to overthrow him amid oil disputes.

1979-1981
Ayatollah Ruhollah Khomeini returns from a decade-long exile to lead the Iran Revolution, attacking the American Embassy and holding 52 hostages for 444 days.

1985-1986
Reagan Administration senior officials secretly facilitate the sale of arms to Iran, even though the country had been restricted since 1979, and diverting funds to Contras, U.S.-backed insurgents in Nicaragua.

1988
The Navy's USS Vincennes mistakenly shoots down an Iran Air Flight passenger plane over the Persian Gulf, killing all 290 people onboard (the U.S. later paid $61.8 million to the victims' families).

2002
Five months after the September 11 terrorist attacks, President George W. Bush labels Iran, Iraq and North Korea the "Axis of Evil" as part of the War on Terror.

2006
The U.S. accuses Iran of funding Iraqi terrorist groups, resulting in sanctions on Iranian banks doing business with American banks.

2015
The Obama administration agrees to lift sanctions on Iran that have devastated its economy, in exchange for the surrender of its nuclear capabilities and allowing the UN to carry out periodic inspections.

2019
Trump publicly brands Iran's elite military, the Islamic Revolutionary Guard Corps, a "terrorist" organization. In response, Iran declares the U.S. a "state sponsor of terrorism."

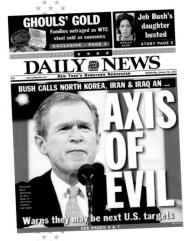

GHOULS' GOLD
Families outraged as WTC steel sold as souvenirs
EXCLUSIVE — PAGE 3

Jeb Bush's daughter busted
NOELLE BUSH
STORY PAGE 5

DAILY NEWS
New York's Hometown Newspaper

BUSH CALLS NORTH KOREA, IRAN & IRAQ AN ...

AXIS OF EVIL

Warns they may be next U.S. targets
SEE PAGES 6 & 7

STATE OF EM

AS THE CORONAVIRUS RAVAGED THE WORLD, PRESIDENT TRUMP LED AN

AT THE START OF 2020, TRUMP'S America seemed destined for continued success, as he looked ahead to reelection. But within weeks, the nation was blindsided by a global pandemic that threatened not only the thriving economy—but most importantly, the lives of millions of citizens. The coronavirus first popped up in Wuhan, China, in December 2019, and rapidly spread throughout the world, with the first U.S. case of COVID-19 confirmed on January 20.

Immediately, Trump established a task force of top infectious-disease experts, led by Vice President Mike Pence, "to monitor, contain and mitigate the spread of the virus," announced then-White House press secretary Stephanie Grisham. "The president's top priority is the health and welfare of the American people."

As scientists raced to develop a vaccine, the Trump administration did all it could to stop the pandemic. Travel restrictions were placed on foreign nationals entering the U.S. from China, Iran, the United Kingdom, Ireland and 26 other European countries. Additionally, Americans returning home from those regions were required to submit to a health screening and 14-day quarantine. But as the disease advanced at an alarming rate, Trump had to ramp up efforts. On March 6, he signed the Coronavirus Preparedness and Response Supplemental Appropriations Act, which provided $8.3 billion to fight the pandemic. As panic set in across the country, schools closed, restaurants suspended dine-in service, major sporting events were canceled and non-essential businesses—like bars, gyms, salons and movie theaters—were shut.

Just a week later, as the number of U.S. cases hit thousands (with 41 confirmed dead), the president declared a national state of emergency to free up $50 billion in federal resources. "It could get worse," warned Trump. "The next eight weeks are critical." In the meantime, major cities and states imposed mandatory lockdowns, beginning with California, New York and Illinois, ordering residents to stay home and go into isolation for the foreseeable future.

But the life-saving measure also devastated the economy. At the

ERGENCY

UNPRECEDENTED EFFORT TO PROTECT AMERICANS FROM THE DEADLY DISEASE.

SUPPLY AND DEMAND

Health-care facilities faced a shortage of protective equipment and ventilators, so FEMA airlifted critical supplies from every part of the globe.

RACE FOR A CURE

In March, Dr. Anthony Fauci gave Trump a tour of the National Institutes of Health's Vaccine Research Center in Bethesda, Maryland.

end of 2019, Trump had managed to get unemployment down to 3.5 percent, the lowest in 50 years. Amid the coronavirus crisis, with people unable to work (in addition to business closures resulting in mass layoffs), that number skyrocketed to nearly 13 percent, as 10 million jobless claims were filed in the last two weeks of March 2020 alone. And it could only get worse, according to economists who predicted the highest unemployment levels since the Great Depression, which was 24.9 percent (by comparison, unemployment during the 2007-2009 recession reached 10 percent).

The strength of the economy has been one of Trump's crowning achievements, and the president acted quickly to prevent an epic fallout. On March 27, as the number of confirmed U.S. cases exceeded 100,000 (with 1,588 deaths), Trump signed the Coronavirus Aid, Relief and Economic Security Act (CARES Act), an unprecedented $2 trillion

stimulus bill that provides assistance to workers, families, and small and large businesses, as well as state governments and hospitals. Per the CARES Act, which passed unanimously in the Senate, eligible individuals could receive as much as $1,200 (plus another $500 for each dependent child) to cover

immediate financial needs during the crisis. "It's twice as large as any relief ever signed," Trump said from the Oval Office. "I want to thank Republicans and Democrats for coming together, setting aside their differences, and putting America first."

As coronavirus spread like wildfire across the U.S., health-care facilities were overwhelmed with the multitude of ill patients, resulting in severe shortages of personal protective equipment (PPE), like masks and gloves, to safeguard medical staff from the highly contagious disease. Complicating matters: While the majority of cases are mild to moderate, thousands progressed to pneumonia, as COVID-19 can attack the respiratory system—and there were only 12,700 ventilators available in the country. In response, Trump invoked the Defense Production Act, giving him the power to order private businesses to prioritize the

APOCALYPSE NOW

As Americans prepared for quarantine, store shelves were wiped clean of most food items, in addition to hand sanitizer, toilet paper and cleaning supplies.

production of necessary resources. Under the DPA, General Motors immediately began manufacturing critical-care ventilators (10,000 per month) and Level 1 face masks (50,000 per day), as needed during the global pandemic. Additionally, Trump arranged for 3M to import 166.5 million masks primarily from its manufacturing facility in China to support U.S. health-care workers.

In the hardest-hit areas, such as New York, New Jersey and Connecticut, Trump deployed over 3,000 military and public-health professionals. And in Manhattan, the epicenter of the virus, the Navy's hospital ship *USNS Comfort* was stationed, at first to treat non-coronavirus patients, but later opened to COVID-19 patients. "Our warriors in this life-and-death battle," noted President Trump, "are the incredible doctors and nurses and health-care workers on the front line of the fight."

But it was the duty of all Americans to slow the spread. And as the U.S. surpassed 800,000 confirmed COVID-19 cases with more than 44,000 dead, social-distancing guidelines were extended until at least April 30 in many parts of the country. "I want to thank the American people, most of all, for the selfless sacrifices they're making for our nation," praised Trump. "Sustaining this war effort is—and that's what it is; this is a war effort—is the patriotic duty of every citizen. While we may be more physically distant for a time, we're closer together in the heart and in the spirit. And through this, great national unity is happening."

THE ROAD AHEAD

Once he's done with politics, golf will likely be in the cards.

As Donald Trump got started making America great again, he was already looking ahead to how to keep it that way. Just hours after he was inaugurated as the 45th president of the United States on January 20, 2017, he filed documents for his 2020 campaign with the Federal Election Commission, and fundraising efforts began immediately to finance Keep America Great.

But while Trump was laser-focused on the November 3, 2020, election and he may not have to think about returning to civilian life for a while, others have been wondering what POTUS will be looking to do after he leaves the White House.

Of course, there's always the (remote) possibility that the normal order of things will change, since Trump's agenda has long been based on shaking things up in Washington. The president even has joked of the left-wing media, "A lot of them say, 'You know he's not leaving' ... So now we have to start thinking about that because it's not a bad idea." But assuming he doesn't overturn the 22nd Amendment that limits presidencies to two terms, what does life after being the most powerful man in the world look like for someone who has worked since he was a teenager?

Even though his three eldest children, Donald Jr., Ivanka and Eric, have a good handle on the family business, it's a safe bet he will still be involved to some extent—at the very least, working on his backswing at one of his 19 Trump Golf courses all over the world. Trump could even return to prime-time television:

It's been reported that he and *The Apprentice* producer Mark Burnett have discussed a number of projects, particularly developing an offshoot of their popular show, tentatively titled *The Apprentice: White House.*

Another possibility is that the president may start his own TV news network, putting his media savvy to work. In 2016, *Vanity Fair* reported that sources close to Trump said he'd discussed launching his own "mini-media conglomerate."

One thing that won't be news is how much Donald Trump has enjoyed fighting for the American people. As he's said, "I had such an easy life. People say, I had such an easy life. Who the hell knew it was going to be this difficult, but I love it."

Donald J. Trump ✓
@realDonaldTrump

9:32 PM · Jan 2, 2020 · Twitter for iPhone

Donald J. Trump ✓
@realDonaldTrump

People are proud to be saying Merry Christmas again. I am proud to have led the charge against the assault of our cherished and beautiful phrase. MERRY CHRISTMAS!!!!!

9:56 PM · Dec 24, 2017 · Twitter for iPhone

Donald J. Trump ✓
@realDonaldTrump

TODAY WE MAKE AMERICA GREAT AGAIN!

6:43 AM · Nov 8, 2016 · Twitter for Android

Donald J. Trump ✓
@realDonaldTrump

How long did it take your staff of 823 people to think that up--and where are your 33,000 emails that you deleted?

Hillary Clinton ✓ @HillaryClinton · Jun 9, 2016
Delete your account. twitter.com/realDonaldTrum...

#WINNING

THE PRESIDENT IS JUST AS ENTERTAINING ON SOCIAL MEDIA AS HE IS IN REAL LIFE: A COMPILATION OF HIS MOST MEMORABLE TWEETS.

Donald J. Trump ✓
@realDonaldTrump

North Korean Leader Kim Jong Un just stated that the "Nuclear Button is on his desk at all times." Will someone from his depleted and food starved regime please inform him that I too have a Nuclear Button, but it is a much bigger & more powerful one than his, and my Button works!

7:49 PM · Jan 2, 2018 · Twitter for iPhone

Donald J. Trump ✓
@realDonaldTrump

My Twitter account was taken down for 11 minutes by a rogue employee. I guess the word must finally be getting out-and having an impact.

6:51 AM · Nov 3, 2017 · Twitter for iPhone

Donald J. Trump ✓
@realDonaldTrump

NO MERCY TO TERRORISTS you dumb bastards!

11:47 AM · Apr 21, 2013 · Twitter for Android

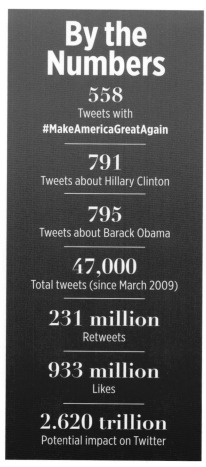

By the Numbers

558
Tweets with #MakeAmericaGreatAgain

791
Tweets about Hillary Clinton

795
Tweets about Barack Obama

47,000
Total tweets (since March 2009)

231 million
Retweets

933 million
Likes

2.620 trillion
Potential impact on Twitter

Donald J. Trump ✓
@realDonaldTrump

For those few people knocking me for tweeting at three o'clock in the morning, at least you know I will be there, awake, to answer the call!

2:37 PM · Sep 30, 2016 · Twitter for Android

Donald J. Trump ✓
@realDonaldTrump

After having written many best selling books, and somewhat priding myself on my ability to write, it should be noted that the Fake News constantly likes to pore over my tweets looking for a mistake. I capitalize certain words only for emphasis, not b/c they should be capitalized!

7:13 PM · Jul 3, 2018 · Twitter for iPhone

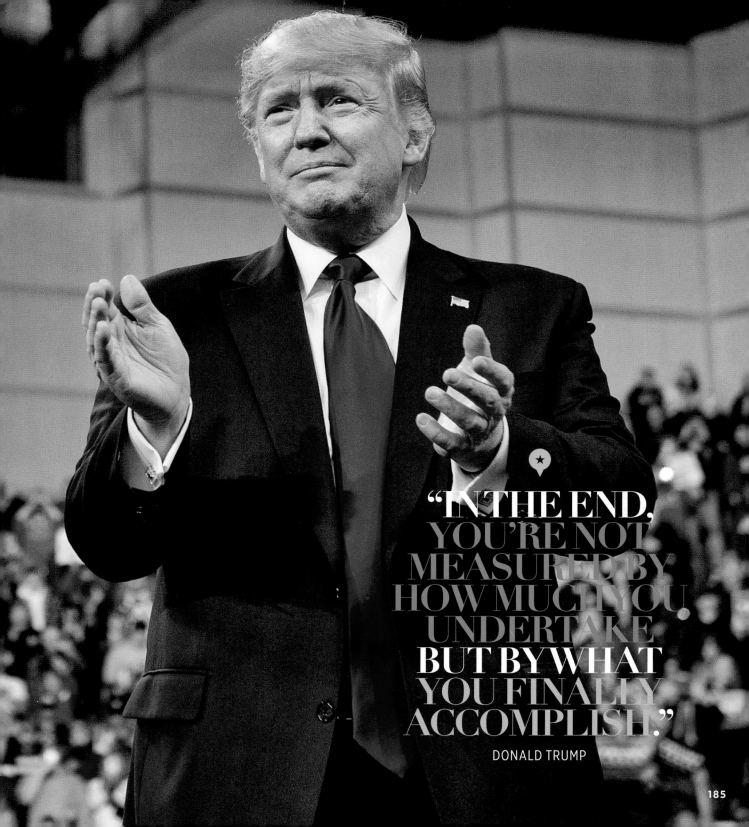

"IN THE END, YOU'RE NOT MEASURED BY HOW MUCH YOU UNDERTAKE BUT BY WHAT YOU FINALLY ACCOMPLISH."

DONALD TRUMP

185

COVER David Hume Kennerly/Getty Images **INSIDE FRONT FLAP** Andrew Harnik/AP Photo **SPINE** Chip Somodevilla/ Getty Images **2–3** Evan Vucci/AP/Shutterstock **4–5** From left: Andrew Harnik/AP Photo; Seth Poppel/Yearbook Library; Mel Melcon/Getty Images; Jim Bourg - Pool/Getty Images **6–7** Andrew Harnik/AP Photo **8–9** Alamy **10** Ted Thai/Getty Images **11** Mario Suriani/AP/Shutterstock **12** Bob Sacha/Getty Images **13** WILBUR FUNCHES/AP Photo; New York Post Archives/Getty Images **14–15** Joe McNally/Getty Images **16** MARTY LEDERHANDLER/AP Photo **17** Joe McNally/Getty Images **18** Nancy Kaye/Getty Images **19** Steve Azzara/Corbis/Getty Images; Davidoff Studios Photography/Getty Images **20** Alamy **21** Slaven Vlasic/Getty Images **22** Mark Wallheiser/Getty Images **23** Mark Wilson/Getty Images; NICHOLAS KAMM/Getty Images **24** Chip Somodevilla/Getty Images **25** Alamy **26** D Dipasupil/Getty Images **27** Joe Raedle/Getty Images **28** Eva Marie Uzcategui T./Anadolu Agency/Getty Images **29** Richard Pohle/Getty Images **30–31** Andrew Harnik/AP Photo **32** John Locher/AP/Shutterstock **33** Evan Vucci/AP Photo **34** Seth Poppel/Yearbook Library **36** Alamy **37** realdonaldtrump/Instagram (2) **38** Seth Poppel/Yearbook Library; Alamy **39–42** Seth Poppel/Yearbook Library (4) **44** Dennis Caruso/NY Daily News Archive/ Getty Images **45** Jack Smith/NY Daily News Archive/Getty Images **46** Seth Poppel/Yearbook Library (2) **47** Frank Russo/NY Daily News Archive/Getty Images **48–49** Ted Thai/The LIFE Picture Collection/Getty Images **50** Richard Drew/AP Photo; Shutterstock; Alamy **51** Harry Hamburg/NY Daily News/Getty Images **52** Jeffrey Asher/Getty Images **53** Marty Lederhandle/AP Photo **54** NY Daily News Archive/Getty Images **55** Clockwis from top left: Raymond Boyd/Michael Ochs Archives/Getty Images; Jeff J Mitchell/Getty Images; The Yomiuri Shimbun/AP Images; Stephen Lovekin/ WireImage; Wilfredo Lee/AP/Shutterstock; Steve Helber/AP/Shutterstock; Tony Ward/Mirrorpix/Getty Images; Wilfredo Lee/AP/Shutterstock **56** Leif Skoogfors/CORBIS/Corbis/Getty Images **57** Jeffrey Asher/Getty Images **58–59** Joe McNally/Getty Images **60** Joe McNally/Getty Images **61** John Roca/NY Daily News Archive/Getty Images; Davidoff Studios/Getty Images **62–63** Ted Thai/The LIFE Picture Collection/Getty Images; AP Photo/Marty Lederhandler **64–65** Clockwise from top left: Alamy; Shutterstock; Evelyn Hockstein/The Washington Post/Getty Images; Alamy (3); Chris Condon/Getty Images **66** Mel Melcon/Getty Images **67** TIMOTHY A. CLARY/Getty Images **68–69** Mary Ellen Matthews/NBC/ Getty Images; Timothy Fadek/Corbis/Getty Image **70–71** Clockwise from left: Jeffrey Asher/Getty Images; Vince Bucci/Getty Images; Mary Ellen Matthews/NBC/Getty Images; Alamy **72–73** Bill Tompkins/Getty Image **74–75** From left:David T. Foster III/Charlotte Observer/Getty Images; Jeff Bottari/AP/ Shutterstock; Paramount Pictures; GABRIEL BOUYS/AFP/Getty Images **77** Ron Galella/Getty Images **78** Sonia Moskowitz/Getty Images **79** BRUCHET Patrick/Paris Match/ Getty Images; Joe McNally/Getty Images **80** Sonia Moskowitz/Getty Images **81** Ron Galella, Ltd./WireImage **82–83** Clockwise from top: Ron Galella/WireImage; Jeff Vespa/WireImage; Evan Agostini/Getty Images; Patrick McMullan/Getty Images; Robin Platzer/The LIFE Images Collection/Getty Images; The LIFE Picture Collection/Getty Images; Mondadori Portfolio/Getty Images **84** Art Zelin/Getty Images **85** David M. Benett/Dave Benett/Getty Images; Adam Taylor/ABC/Getty Images **86** Rose Hartman/Getty Images **87** Karin Cooper/Liaison/Getty Images **88–89** Clockwise from right: Sylvain Gaboury/ FilmMagic; John Barrett/Shutterstock; Alamy **90–91** Clockwise from top: Karl Feile/Hulton Archive/Getty Images; Julien Mattia/NurPhoto/Getty Images; Alex Wong/Getty Images; James Devaney/WireImage; Davidoff Studios/ Getty Images; IPAK Images/Polaris **92** Davidoff Studios/Getty Images **94** Amanda Schwab/Starpix/Shutterstock **95** Brad Barket/Getty Images **96–97** Christopher Gregory/Getty Images **98** David Becker/Getty Images **99** Ron Galella, Ltd./WireImage; Cindy Ord/Getty Images **100–101** Clockwise from left: Chris Kleponis/Getty Images; BRENDAN SMIALOWSKI/Getty Images; Ron Galella, Ltd./Getty Images; Lev Radin/Pacific Press/Getty Images **102** Aaron P. Bernstein/Getty Images **103** Sonia Moskowitz/Getty Images; Tom Gates/Getty Images **104** Michael Tercha/Chicago Tribune/Getty Images **105** Brian Marcus/Fred Marcus Photography/Getty Images; Alex Wong/Getty

CENTENNIAL BOOKS

An Imprint of
Centennial Media, LLC
40 Worth St., 10th Floor
New York, NY 10013, U.S.A.

CENTENNIAL BOOKS is a trademark of Centennial Media, LLC

ISBN 978-1-951274-32-0
Distributed by
Simon & Schuster, Inc.
1230 Avenue of the Americas
New York, NY 10020, U.S.A.

For information about custom editions, special sales and premium and corporate purchases,
please contact Centennial Media at contact@centennialmedia.com.

Manufactured in Malaysia

Publishers & Co-Founders Ben Harris, Sebastian Raatz
Creative Director Jessica Power
Art Directors Natali Suasnavas, Joseph Ulatowski
Assistant Art Director Jaclyn Loney
Photo Editor Christina Creutz
Production Manager Paul Rodina
Production Assistant Alyssa Swiderski
Editorial Assistant Tiana Schippa
Sales & Marketing Jeremy Nurnberg